BOB DYLAN
An Illustrated History

BOB DYLAN
An Illustrated History

Produced by Michael Gross
with a text by Robert Alexander

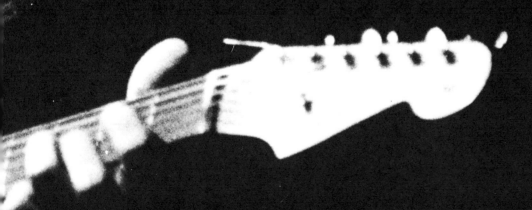

Elm Tree Books/London

Photograph on title page © Diana Davies/Nancy Palmer Photo Agency, Inc.

The cover: Bob Dylan in 1965 by Jerrold Schatzberb.
Designed by Marcia Ben-Eli
Copyright © 1978 by Michael Gross
First published in Great Britain 1978 by
Elm Tree Books/Hamish Hamilton Ltd
90 Great Russell Street, London WC1B 3PT
Second impression July 1978
ISBN: 0-241-10038-0
Printed and bound in Great Britain by
Hollen Street Press Ltd at Slough, Berkshire

Contents

Acknowledgments

Many people contribute to a scrapbook such as the one you hold in your hands—far too many to mention here. Of special note, though, are the fine photographers whose works grace this volume. Jim Marshall should be singled out here for his irreplaceable contribution of twenty previously unpublished photos of Bob Dylan, from his arrival in New York in 1961 to his Johnny Cash show appearance in 1969.

Julian Neal, Bob and Larry Goldberg, Mary at Columbia Studios, David Braun, Mark Senderoff, Alan Bomser, Peggy Martin, Barry Levine, Jaan Uhelszki, Jann Ricca, Jed Mattes, and especially Jimmy Optner, Ellen Levine, Perry Knowlton, and Ellen Dwyer also deserve personal thanks for a variety of reasons.

Toby Thompson, the journalist who first traced Bob Dylan's roots back to Hibbing in his work *Positively Main Street: An Unorthodox View of Bob Dylan* must be singled out for his gracious permission to use portions of his book as the basis of the North Country chapter. Michael Ochs, Billy James, Murray Krugman, Michael Zilkha, Brian Stibal (editor of *TBZB,* the Dylan fanzine), Sandy Gant (compiler of an unequaled Dylan discography), Alan Weberman, Tim Hogan, James Day, and Andrew Lamy contributed knowledge and memorabilia. Gerard Malanga, Ike Gellis, Gene Keesee, Jerry Shatzberg and Lynn Goldsmith were instrumental in uncovering the treasure trove of photos.

Robert Alexander's text speaks for itself. He's only asked to add these last words: "Suzette told me Bob Dylan came from outer space. I believe her. You've been warned."

Michael Gross
New York City
January 1978

(Bob Gruen/Elektra/Asylum Records)

To Estelle Gross, Miranda Alexander, Beatty Zimmerman and other Jewish mothers everywhere.

"Yes, well, what can you know about anybody? Book or photographs, they don't tell you too much about a person."

—Bob Dylan

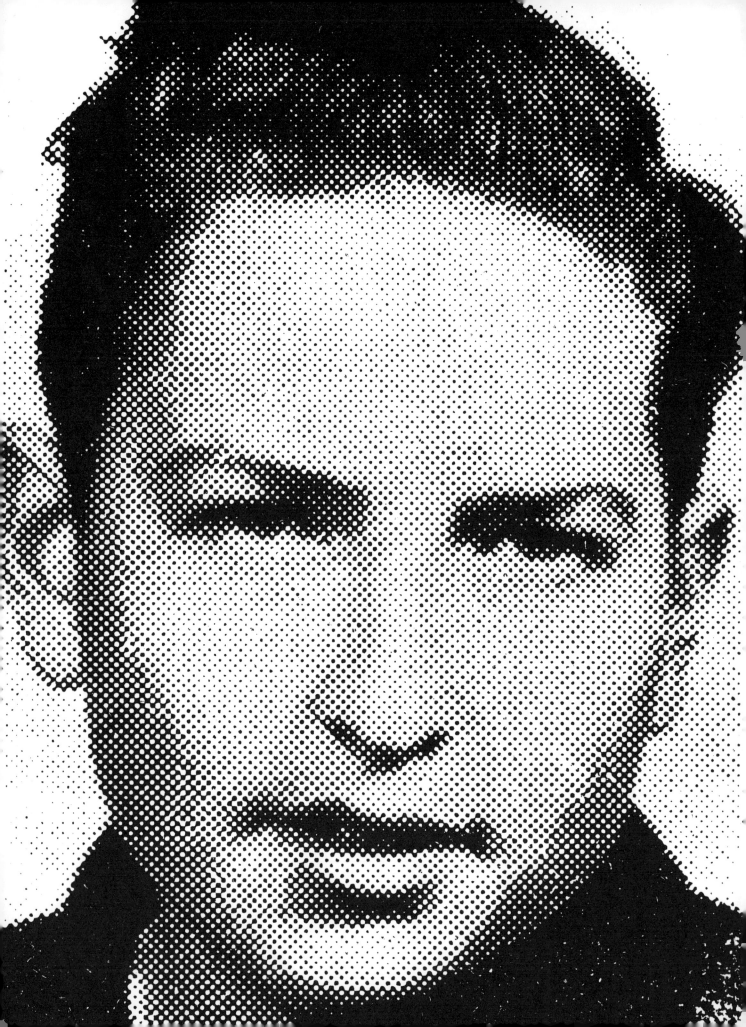

1: The Crossroads of His Doorstep

David Westurn
Laura Wilcox

Dennis Wichman
Michael Winsor

Robert Zimmerman

Betsy Zozgornik

From Hibbing's high school yearbook.

IMAGINE A WORLD in which Bob Dylan had never lived. A world where no one said, "The answer is blown' in the wind." A world where Puff the Magic Dragon never stood accused by finger-pointing tambourine men. A world with two Vietnams, perhaps. A world with the Rolling Stones, but without *Rolling Stone.*

Highway 61 would be an anonymous signpost on a forgotten piece of road, and the lives of Davey Moore, Emmett Till, Hattie Carroll and Rubin Carter would be no more known than yours or mine. Hundreds of writers, singers, songsmiths, musicians and poets from Allen Ginsberg to Harry Belafonte would have led appreciably different lives. Many would have had no careers at all. Hunter Thompson might never have endorsed a peanut farmer for president. That president, Jimmy Carter, might never have been elected. The student rolls of Kent State University might have shown several more graduations. What Bob Dylan called our "empty-handed" armies might still be arrayed around the world. Henry Kissinger's trash would be untouched, garbagology yet a glimmer in some tabloid editor's eye.

The one with the weird voice has etched himself onto this technological age with nothing but the force of words and music. In two decades defined by movement and change, Dylan has managed to move faster, melding the popular with the elitist, reflecting our desires and our myths as much as he exposed the cracks in the rigid standards of The American Ethic—Ma and Pa's vision of the good life, which the generations that grew up after World War II enjoyed in all its abundance, appreciated as the end of the hard road, and still found wanting.

Robert Allen Zimmerman, son of Beatty and Abraham Zimmerman, was born in Duluth, Minnesota, on May 24, 1941, when prosperity and war were poised to march hand-in-hand across America. He grew up in Hibbing,* Minnesota, a town where normality was a goal to be achieved; where there

*I am indebted to Toby Thompson's *Positively Main Street: An Unorthodox View of Bob Dylan,* Coward, McCann & Geoghegan, 1971, for a majority of the material referred to herein concerning Hibbing, Minnesota.

1

was a good section, a bad section, and the tracks in between; a Main Street; some kids you knew would turn out good, some who for sure would turn out bad, and some, like Robert Zimmerman, about whom you couldn't be positive.

Hibbing, where the Zimmermans moved when Bob was six, was not a bad place to grow up in. Bob was the son of a merchant, an appliance salesman in a town dominated by its major group of settlers, about 20,000 European Catholic immigrants. They were basic working folk for whom conformity was a fact, not an option. It was a town where their open mine pit, a five-hundred-foot-deep, three-mile-long gouge, was a disgrace as well as a local tourist attraction with built-in viewing sites.

Of course the pit had a history behind it; its climbs and falls mirrored the town's own fortunes. Originally a logging town, Hibbing's brush with the future came when Frank Hibbing discovered red iron ore there in 1893. In 1913, Greyhound Bus Lines was founded there. In 1919, the Bookmobile was invented to serve the miners slaving away at the nearby Mesabi Range. Throughout the First World War, prosperity was the town's motto. After the war, the Oliver Mining Company appeared on the scene and took the entire town 1½ miles south in a four-year move in order to open new mining areas. When the Depression hit, Hibbing suffered, and when the Second World War came, even though the mines returned to peak operation at about the time of Bob's birth, their severe depletion promised hard times ahead.

In 1945, Bob's younger brother David was born. The family lived in a rectangular flat-roofed home of light tan stucco at 2425 East 7th Avenue. It was a solid home with no pretensions, a good home for good people, with pine walls, breakfast nook, dining room, big kitchen, rec room in the basement. Bob and David shared a bedroom.

In 1951, Bob's father brought home an inexpensive piano. Bob took a lesson and gave up while David became the musical Zimmerman son. Bob painted word pictures on paper and kept a low profile. At an early age, though, he taught himself piano, harmonica, guitar, and autoharp. He often went to the movies alone.

Hibbing was a depressing mining town with bars full of cracked-up alkies, union men and scabs with bad memories, men too old or too tired to care. But there was one bright spot, Crippas, Hibbing's local music store. Here young Zimmerman was a semi-regular, first listening to classical music but by eighth grade graduating to blues, country and western, and primitive 50s rock and roll. Here he began to reach out of himself and his desolation to escape Hibbing's grinding environment. It might have been the romantic escape the bluesmen talked about on the rails, or that longing to be free their voices echoed, but their message hit home in the young man's developing consciousness. By now he was carrying his Sears, Roebuck guitar everywhere and listening to the radio late into the night, when faraway stations played faraway music.

In his freshman year of high school he formed his first band called The Golden Chords. They practiced in the living room or in the garage playing basic rhythm and blues, Little Richard songs, almost anything the radio carried. While the rest of the country was reacting against this uncouth invasion of the airways, Bob was revelling in it. How else to be outrageous in a place where outrage was forbidden by mutual consent. He put together another band and bought his first motorcycle, a big Harley Davidson 74, and painted it black. Having a cycle and roaring around town was one way

to raise a few eyebrows. Playing notorious rock and roll was another. He was, even at that time, a study in contrasts.

Abe Zimmerman with John Sebastian, Duluth, November 1966. *(Joseph Stevens/Photo Trends)*

On the one hand he was remembered by his high school mates as quiet, serious and an introvert. He sat in the front row in English, his best subject. He dressed sharp and clean. He got Bs and B+s and never cut class. He was in Latin Club in his sophomore year and Social Studies Club as a senior. He went to the Agudath Achim Synagogue and on Sundays he'd dress up for the big family dinner. All very normal on the outside, and the only thing he ever got excited about was music. Since he couldn't escape Hibbing physically, he ran away in his mind and played electric music until it was easy to see he'd be a rock star or a little of himself would wither up and die inside. It was music that led him onward, music and his first girlfriend, Echo Helstrom.

Echo met Bob at the L & B cafe in town when they were both in the eleventh grade. She was from a tougher part of town, and thought he was a goody-goody because he always appeared so quiet in school. Then she saw him under a streetlight playing his guitar. They talked and discovered they listened to the same faraway radio stations, which broadcast from Little Rock and Chicago with DJs like Gatemouth Page. Bob's eyes got wider and wider as they talked about Chuck Berry's "Maybelline" and Fats Domino, Jimmy Reed and Little Richard. At last there was a soulmate in that dead empty town!

They were brought together because of their mutual need to escape. Bob wanted to be a rock star, Echo, an actress. She was attracted by his strange reserve—he didn't attempt to kiss her on the mouth for a month after they met. Bob seemed to Echo to be upset about his Judaism. He also told her he wanted to change his last name to Dylan, after the poet Dylan Thomas.

Bob and Echo may have been an item for local gossip, but his first love was still the blues, which he played passionately with his new band. And they played everywhere and anywhere—from school shows to youth club outings. Yes, he'd play anywhere and LOUD—much too loud for this desolation row in the middle of the country. It all went along with his new tough punk image, the rebel on the road (although he did sell his cycle after almost running down a child).

Still Bob's fascination with the blues deepened, eventually winning out over his affair with Echo. He tried different singing styles and sought out "colored people" (although few passed through lily-white Hibbing)—anything for a shot of real rhythm and blues. In the spring of '57, Abraham, Bob's father, sensing his eldest's restlessness, finally consented to allow him to take the bus to Minneapolis. Once Bob got a taste of the road, he would never come home again.

2: God on His Side

As a freshman at the University of Minnesota, Bob took the name Dylan, and began to perform at local clubs. *(Photo Trends)*

BY THE TIME Bob Zimmerman graduated from Hibbing High on June 5, 1959, his double life was ending. He had established his "greaser" image among the town locals with his wild ways, his Harley, and his rock and roll. Now he was to pick up an independent identity as an eighteen-year-old freshman in the arts college of the University of Minnesota in Minneapolis.

In the fall of '59, Bob began to burrow further into country and western music, cowboy songs, hillbilly music, and the rapidly developing urban folk scene that had its own set of champions in Dinkytown, the student quarter of Minneapolis near the university. At first Bob lived at the Sigma Alpha Mu (Sammy) fraternity house and tried to fit into the collegiate atmosphere—the Ivy League button-down look. But soon enough, he discovered the Dinkytown scene, a heavy if dated Bohemia modeled after the Beat Culture, then on its last legs. He started hanging out at a little club called the Ten O'Clock Scholar, a block from campus. They played folk music there; Bob told the proprietor he wanted to be a folksinger too.

Bob was still secretive about his past. After all, he was the son of a middle-class Jewish merchant, in the midst of a slick college environment. To compensate for his square background he intricately layered the facts of his life with the fictions he imagined of a more glamorous life. It was to be his characteristic trademark years later, after he became famous. And the characters Bob invented were so incredible and vital, they had to be real. Later on when he went to New York, that trail of incredible stories would spin out more. He started in Dinkytown by calling himself Bob Dylan.

The stories he continued to tell, first in Dinkytown and later on as his fame increased, have been repeated in books and magazine articles. Few of them were true, but the myths Dylan created were his way of filling out an image, and thus were crucial. Whether with interviewers, record company executives, or even friends, he'd say that he had run away from home seven times by the age of eighteen. First at ten, to Chicago—where he met a black street musician who taught him to play the spoons. At twelve, to Evanston, Illinois, where he met bluesman Big Joe Williams. At thirteen, he said he'd joined a carnival touring the Dakotas and Minnesota. At fifteen he ran away twice—once to New Mexico, and once to California where he claimed varying degrees of intimacy with Woody Guthrie. In response to both his need for acceptance and the heavy anti-Semitism of Minneapolis, Dylan developed a tough shell. He even went as far as to tell people he was an Okie orphan—anything so they'd never know and he'd always remain an enigma.

As it was, the Sammy house was no place for a young man anxious to hide his roots, so after a short stretch of interest in school, he moved out. He started hanging out on 4th Street, Dinkytown's main drag, where The Scholar, The Bastille, and the folk music scene dominated. Leather, motorcycles, rock and roll music were uncool there. Folk music was happening—it got you attention and it got you laid. To the young Bob Dylan who, with his need for fame, used to claim to be Bobby Vee, it was the path to growing up. Horny, headstrong, rebellious, as undiscriminating as any man who's discovered his "little boy" guise works with women, Dylan was doing nothing but stretching out. He was sowing some oats and creating the identity that allowed him room to move, room to be a stray, room to learn.

It was a period more characterized by study than success. He was tired of school within a month, but remained infatuated with the city and his new role as an itinerant (if inarticulate) Jewish folksinger, as self-styled critics were already calling him. Within the Dinkytown subculture were people with roots in the folk tradition; through them he was introduced to all the then-current folk singers from Pete Seeger and The Weavers (blacklisted folksingers harassed by the House Un-American Activities Committee) to Memphis and Chicago blues, to dusty Woody Guthrie ballads, to the rags and hollers from the mountains of Appalachia. He still told tall tales of his rock star roots, but not around his new folkie cohorts. Visits to Hibbing were transformed into pilgrimages down home to Oklahoma.

The few times he played for free in various coffeehouses in his off-key nasal monotone, he drove customers into the streets. Soon enough though, he was offered a two-dollar-a-night gig at The Purple Onion, and later played at The Scholar. He'd already burned his bridges at the university and, though officially enrolled for three semesters, through mid-1960, he soon stopped going to class altogether.

Bob found a small group of new friends, pre-New Left, pre-SDS radicals who gave him a sense of political direction and a generally supportive atmosphere in which to pursue his own interest in the less commercial kinds of folk music then growing in popularity. He was young enough not to care about money, clothes or anything else save shelter from his storms. And it was the music that pushed him onward.

The stories he told made the truth virtually irrelevant. He was a charming waif all in all. He played the role of ramblin' boy with such conviction that those who came near him felt no reason to question the obvious holes in his tales. He was like a young, slightly mad, constantly moving little-boy-lost with a developing sense of humor and timing that could show through both charm and sarcasm. His style seemed to come as much from Charlie Chaplin as from James Dean, and if the combination sounds strange, it was in the tension between the two that he began to find his own power and carve out an identity.

During the summer of 1960, while John F. Kennedy and Richard M. Nixon were battling for the presidency, one of Bob's early friends turned him on to *Bound for Glory,* the autobiography of one of America's folk greats, Woody

Guthrie. In one day, he went from a Guthrie fan to Guthrie fanatic. He started to copy Woody's reedy, throaty style, and when few challenged his stories of meeting Woody, he embellished them more. With Woody's persona incorporated into his own, Dylan had the psychic baggage he needed to separate himself from "everybody else."

He grew more arrogant, and more aware of his growing power. Every party became a Dylan concert. In the fall of 1960, when John Kennedy's talk of new frontiers and moving with vigor began to seem believable to all Americans, Dylan was on the road to fame and fortune. He had no home in Minneapolis anyway, living the life of a tramp in cheap apartments and singing at local hoots.

Though Woody was dying in East Orange, New Jersey, his music gained new life in the early Sixties. The climate could not have left young Bob Dylan untouched. Besides, now he knew the way to go. By November, with Kennedy elected and the gray Eisenhower years over, Dylan still worked the coffeehouses, but his heart and mind were set on New York City and Woody.

Bob told all who'd listen he was going to the Big Apple to strike it rich and see his idol, but no one in that bohemian ivory tower of Dinkytown believed him. They thought he was deluding himself. Not entirely. One morning in December, Bob tried to call Woody at Greystone Hospital in East Orange where he was slowly dying from Huntington's chorea. He couldn't get through because the doctors there said Woody was too sick to talk to anyone. That same evening Bob packed his knapsack, slung his guitar around his shoulder and split from Dinkytown. It would be poetic to say he walked out on the highway, stuck out his thumb, and headed East for fame and fortune. The truth, though more mundane, is just as interesting. He headed north to Hibbing where he got his parents' approval for his "new identity" and enough money to get to New York. With his parents blessings, Woody Guthrie as his muse, and Greystone Hospital as his destination, he hit the road.

He was not yet twenty.

His journey took him from Hibbing to New York by way of Chicago and, backtracking once, Madison, Wisconsin. He had his image down pat: holes in his shoes, blisters on his thumb, Huck Finn slouch hat over a reddish brown scraggly mop of hair, and the face of a Jewish angel. And he had his need: to pay tribute to his idol and follow his chosen path. He'd gotten Woody's talking blues down and his tall tales were getting wilder by the minute. Most of the time they seemed to work. With nowhere to stay, no repertoire to speak of aside from his Guthrie songs, and a rap about traveling wearing thin, Bob finally hit the snowy streets of New York City in late January 1961.

In Greenwich Village a new energy was stirring. Dylan must have felt it because that's where he headed, wandering MacDougal and Bleecker streets with his guitar and his sack. He knew he could sing better than everyone else.

Now he'd prove it.

3: The Hour of the Ship

Backstage on his first appearance at Town Hall in 1962. (© *1977 Jim Marshall*)

GOING TO NEW York to see Woody, Dylan was unknowingly on his way to the city where Woody's successors had become the Beats in the late Fifties. Reacting against the war in Korea, the knuckling-under of the intelligentsia to "Tailgunner" Joe McCarthy and his list-waving pink hysteria, the continuing threat of atomic annihilation, and the plastic culture of the Eisenhower administration, the Beats had come to a literate form of protest that caused as much horror to the entrenched minions of society as the Beatles' admissions of LSD-taking would almost a decade later.

The Beats spread from Greenwich Village to San Francisco's North Beach and then slowly back across America again, as their need to howl against the Silent Generation, their exaltations of sex, drugs, the Road, Zen Buddhism, Negroes, jazz, and their denunciation of the established rules of syntax, song and American Logic disseminated into the younger minds of the land. Minds like that of Bob Dylan, who knew the difference when Jack Kerouac, the Beats' hitchhiker saint, explained, "Beat means beatitude, not beat up."

Or as Dean Moriarity put it, "The only people for me are the mad ones, the ones who are mad to live, mad to talk, mad to be saved, desirous of everything at the same time, the ones who never yawn or say a commonplace thing, but burn, burn, burn like fabulous roman candles."

In the West, Ken Kesey, soon to be the author of *One Flew Over the Cuckoo's Nest,* was nearing the end of his transformation from Beat Author to Electric Kool Aid Prankster. All across the country, the young people who'd spent the Fifties admiring the Negro were being told to put up or shut up. As the Silents faded like old soldier Eisenhower, the successors of the Beats were converging on New York, where attention was being paid to the work-shirted young men and women "discovering" the American Folk Tradition.

The Beats, writing directly from the experience of their contemporaries, had lessened the gulf between art and real life. With John F. Kennedy, politics could again be seen by the young as a part of life and thus a fitting subject for art. And if art had knuckled under to the frustrating blandness of the Fifties, then where better to find it than in the parts of America that had resisted modernity: Appalachia, the Dust Bowl, the places where people remembered famous anarchist "Red" Emma Goldman, the Wobblies (Industrial Workers of the World), and labor organizer Joe Hill as heroes and heroines.

Joan Baez was a dominant figure in the small scene Dylan found in Greenwich Village, and her position was indicative of where it was at. She was a folk conservative, daughter of a research physicist, who'd begun singing in Boston coffeehouses and made her first major appearance at the Newport Folk Festival in Newport, Rhode Island, in 1959. Students, like those who gave her her start in Boston and Cambridge, comprised the vanguard of whatever "folk movement" could be said to have then existed.

The music Baez played, while evocative, was not current. Much of it had been catalogued in the 1890s by a Harvard musicologist. "Barbara Allen" and "Mary Hamilton," violent, depressing songs of medieval times, and traditional American songs like "Wildwood Flower" struck a chord among her young audiences who, having escaped both the Fifties and the American educational system relatively unscathed, were in the process of discovering such new feelings as idealism and worldliness. Peripherally involved with such movements as civil rights and banning the bomb, the folk singers still appeared to be above the fray, their contemporary material often being songs about the Depression and the Dust Bowl—songs made famous by the likes of Woody Guthrie. Pete Seeger and the Weavers made underground classics after McCarthy's blacklisting kept them from national prominence. They were revived after the Senator's death in 1957. Hootenannies, group sings, and a liberalism new to campuses gave rise to new folkies like the Kingston Trio, and new life to the careers of Guthrie followers like Ramblin' Jack Elliot (Elliot Charles Adnopoz; son of a Brooklyn doctor, he had actually gone "on the road" with Woody) and Black bluesmen on whose music much of both folk and rock was based.

That conservative folk scene was based in New York at least partially because Woody Guthrie had chosen to live out his last days there. Sick for ten years on and off by 1961, Woody was in bad shape. His friends like Seeger, Ramblin' Jack, Peter La Farge, Will Geer and Cisco Houston stuck nearby, often joining Woody on weekends at the East Orange, New Jersey, home of Bob and Sid Gleason, for whole days of talk and song. Though crippled by Huntington's disease, Guthrie would still do his best to play and sing with them.

During January, Dylan made several approaches into Guthrie's scene. He visited the hospital in central Jersey and the Guthrie home in Howard Beach, Queens. Through much persistence Dylan managed to gain admittance into that charmed circle. Over the next several weeks a rapport grew between the dying troubadour and his fan from Hibbing. Guthrie was charmed by the ragamuffin kid. He wasn't sure Dylan would make it as a writer, but he was quickly convinced of Bob's talents as a singer.

Meanwhile, in New York, Bob was taking the first steps toward the career he wanted. One night he wandered into the Folklore Center, a store and meeting place run by Israel Young (known as Izzy to his friends, which included all of the Village folk scene). Bob's first New York folk vision was of a girl playing "Pastures of Plenty" on the banjo. Later he played at the Folklore Center, and the *Village Voice* described him in the MacDougal Street shop playing autoharp, "mumbling" a song about a Captain Gray. They

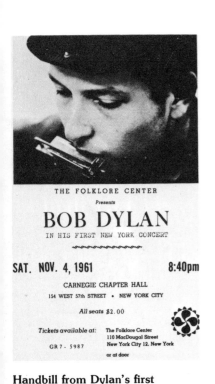

THE FOLKLORE CENTER

Presents

BOB DYLAN
IN HIS FIRST NEW YORK CONCERT

SAT. NOV. 4, 1961   8:40pm

CARNEGIE CHAPTER HALL
154 WEST 57th STREET • NEW YORK CITY

All seats $2.00

Tickets available at: The Folklore Center
                           110 MacDougal Street
GR 7 - 5987   New York City 12, New York

                           or at door

Handbill from Dylan's first formal appearance.

called him extraordinary and predicted that within a year he would emerge as a talent to be reckoned with. In the meantime he slept wherever he could, even on subways. And he was trying very, very hard to make it. By the middle of February, he was visiting Woody several times a week, his awe increasing along with his confidence in his own talent. More encouraging, however, was that now he was playing an occasional gig at places like the Commons on MacDougal, and beginning to be accepted by the Gods of Folk.

Dylan was running hard and fast on a motherlode of natural talent. He was singing for coffee, food, a dollar a day, going to once-a-week auditions at Gerde's Folk City, the Gaslight and the Bitter End. Still he was a little weird looking, and the coffeehouse managers were telling him, ''Go away, you look like a hillbilly.'' By late February, he was occasionally gigging as an opening act for an opening act, playing for uptowners who ''came down to hear the · freaks'' and the Village crowd he hoped would notice him. Few people would hire him, even as a backup, and though he could be as charming as a salesman of snake oil, the doors that mattered stayed closed.

Several coffeeshops and bars served as his bedroom when he couldn't find a bed, and his automat when he had no coins for food. If he had money he'd stay in flophouses. He did have a talent for getting people to take care of him, especially young women with maternal instincts. Often broke, he'd hitch out to East Orange to see the Gleasons, who had a tremendous record collection and an open refrigerator. His first recordings were made there and include ''San Francisco Bay Blues,'' ''Gypsy Davey,'' ''Pastures of Plenty,'' and ''Jessie James.''

Somewhere along the way, he may have tried to break into the tight little world of rock music 1961. His excursions to such uptown landmarks as the Brill Building didn't come to anything if they occurred; some form of early rejection was evident in both his songs and conversation.

By early April, he was doing it as a professional, having played before a small audience at a New York University Folk Music Society—sponsored show. That same month he discovered the Monday night hoots at Gerde's, a club on West 4th Street run by Mike Porco that had begun presenting folk in 1960. At Gerde's, Dave Van Ronk, Len Chandler, Tom Paxton, Cisco Houston and even Arlo Guthrie, Woody's son, could play to SRO crowds.

Now that he was gaining some renown, Dylan was again doing his New Mexico-orphan-on-the-road numbers to anyone who might believe them. It was nothing Ramblin' Jack, the Jewish cowboy from Ocean Parkway, Brooklyn, hadn't done. Though Bob knew too much to be the Okie he claimed to be, and though when questioned his stories about Arvella Gray, Mance Lipscomb, Carl Perkins, Bobby Vee, Jesse Fuller, and Big Joe Williams usually cracked, few took real offense. He used his carny slang a lot, and talked about how he got his nose from a Sioux uncle. Soon people knew his name, talked it around the Village and came to see him after midnight, when the amateurs and the tourists were gone from the clubs and the folk scene reigned into the night. Motivated, complex, highly competitive, Dylan's already noticed ''arrogance'' was tempered by a fierce need for approval from those he looked up to and those he could learn from.

In April, Porco hired Dylan to open for John Lee Hooker's two-week engagement at Gerde's, despite the fact that Bob was busted flat, underage, and Porco had to sign on as his guardian so he could play under contract.

Backstage at The Bitter End with Pete Seeger, 1963. (© *1977 Jim Marshall)*

Opening night, he played "House of the Rising Sun" and "Song to Woody." Attention was finally being paid and people were being brought to Gerde's to see this new kid. Even Joan Baez and *New York Times* critic Robert Shelton approved. Though his time in New York, leading to this official debut, had often been painful, with Dylan discovering some of the harsher realities and the difference between talk and action, it was an auspicious first gig. At its end he left the city for the first time, partially satisfied he was going somewhere.

In May, he arrived at the Indian Neck Folk Festival in Connecticut where he played a few talking blues but impressed his listeners as being imitative, an asshole, vicious, and very uncool. He also met his future road manager, Bobby Neuwirth, for the first time. At the end of May he was back in Dinkytown where he recorded some of his Gerde's repertoire. His growth must have astounded his friends, as did the first hint of his charisma in the emergence of a personality cult around him. He played his guitar and loved to have an audience. When he left, those who knew him may have felt regret at their loss. For most, though, his singleness of purpose struck them as lack of caring.

Back in the City in June, he began to write with a passion, picking up ideas all around him, filling his pockets with scraps of scribbled paper. He turned incidents like a riot on a Bear Mountain picnic boat excursion into a hilarious talking blues, sometimes well-planned, sometimes improvised on the spot, never to be exactly repeated.

Except for these almost comic routines (aided by his now well-developed Chaplinesque sense of timing and control), his public appearances were still based on traditional material. He was soaking up influences as fast as they came along, building structures on which he could hang his words. Even as he was learning about politics and poets, Rimbaud and Brecht, from older singers like Van Ronk, his image remained that of a slightly dumb hick. On the outside he was a hayseed; underneath the mind was working, reading voraciously, discovering other kinds of performance, like Lord Buckley, the immaculately hip aristocrat who told fables in bop slang. In Cambridge, Massachusetts, in June, he met Ric Von Schmidt, who also taught him songs and techniques.

Bob's first manager was Terri Van Ronk, Dave's wife, who got him his first out-of-town show at Caffé Lena in Saratoga Springs, New York, a spa town that is the home of Skidmore College. Unfortunately the wellbred young ladies talked through his set. At Club 47 in Cambridge (from which Tom Rush would soon emerge) he was considered too weird. At the Second Fret in Philadelphia the audience thought he was a Woody Guthrie clone. Still some success occurred. In June he got a job playing backup harmonica on the title cut of a Harry Belafonte album, *Midnight Special* (Belafonte was then the king of calpyso music). Bob was supposed to work the whole album, but Belafonte was too much of a perfectionist, demanding too many takes on each song to please Bob, the roughhewn hick who took his $50 and split.

In the last days of July, Dylan was invited to appear on a WRVR broadcast from New York's Riverside Church with Ramblin' Jack, Van Ronk, Victoria Spivey and others. He did two songs and a Lord Buckley takeoff monologue called "Poor Lazarus," as well as backing up Danny Kalb, a noted blues guitarist, on harp. He also played a tune with Ramblin' Jack called "Acne." Observers noted how his ability to balance between calculated comedy and apparent lack of preparation caused an electric tension in his performance. He was also beginning to fall in love with Suze Rotolo, a seventeen-year-old beauty he'd been seeing on the fringes of the Village scene, but more about that later on.

Bob was now making frequent trips to Cambridge where he enjoyed the looser atmosphere of the folk scene. In August Bob was called onstage at Club 47, and embarked on a close friendship with singer Caroline Hester and her then-husband Richard Farina. The next month they invited him to play harmonica on her new album. On September 26 he opened at Gerde's again for a two-week stint with the Greenbriar Boys, an ardent group of city-bred bluegrass musicians, and got a writeup in the *New York Times*. He enlarged his relationship with blueswoman Victoria Spivey and Big Joe Williams, with whom she was about to record. Bob asked her if she could use a white harmonica player. The answer was yes and plans were made for him to play in an October recording session.

Columbia Records, in the form of John Hammond, intervened. On September 30, Dylan recorded with Hester, playing backup harp on three cuts for her first Hammond-produced Columbia album. Hammond, a legend in the music business—he had recorded Bessie Smith and Billie Holiday, and had brought such talents as Pete Seeger and Aretha Franklin under the CBS banner—was immediately impressed by Bob and signed him on the spot as a songwriter at the then unprecedented royalty rate of 4 percent. Rumbles reverberated through the Village. Dylan had been signed.

Bob entered Columbia Studios in October of 1961, just him, his guitar, his harmonica and twenty songs. The whole album cost $400. On October 21, Dylan entered the studio with Victoria Spivey and Big Joe Williams. He played some song fragments and the engineer inside wanted him to do more. Dylan averred. If you can't sing, just grunt, said the engineer, trying to adjust the sound levels. Later on when the session was finished and people were filling out W-2 withholding forms, someone asked Dylan what his name was. Bob said Grunt. What? Was that Blind Boy Grunt? asked a musician. Yep, said Bob. Thus Blind Boy Grunt entered the American blues consciousness.

Blind Boy Grunt or no, Dylan was in the big leagues now. Izzy Young planned a concert. Columbia Records was preparing his album for release in early 1962. On November 4, about fifty people sat in the two hundred-seat Carnegie Chapter Hall for Bob's concert debut. Tickets were $2 at the door. Izzy lost money but Bob still made his $20 performance fee. Bob was annoyed that only his friends showed up, though there were other consolations. Now that he was making a little money, he moved from the Lower East Side into a series of apartments and hotels, ending at an $80-a-month flat on West 4th Street, paying the previous tenant $350 of his $1000 CBS advance to buy old furniture. It wasn't much and it was barely home. He wanted his friend Suze to move in with him but she wasn't ready yet. Besides, people were beginning to make demands on Bob's mind. Albert Grossman, his new manager, was one of them.

Grossman had previously managed the Gate of Horn in Chicago and moved to New York to manage Odetta. He then began the star-making process with Peter, Paul and Mary, about to have their first hit with "Lemon Tree," and was already Bob's unofficial mentor, having been introduced to his music through Bob Shelton at the *Times*. Dylan was intrigued by Grossman and asked what Hammond thought of him. Hammond thought Grossman was good enough. He had a reputation as being tough, effective, and a fighter for his artists. The positives outweighed the negatives, Dylan signed a seven-year contract, and Grossman began to reign as manager that would last until just after the recording of *John Wesley Harding*.

In mid-December Dylan split for Minnesota to play at a University of Minnesota Hootenanny and, presumably, spend the holidays with his parents. At the hoot, he played solely Guthrie and Reverend Gary Davis songs. His technical advances were of course noticed. There he recorded a long tape, much of which would surface on the first bootleg record, *The Great White Wonder*, and talked about how great his first album was, how he'd be a star. He saw his old girl Echo, who noted he'd lost his baby fat, and asked him why he wasn't playing rock 'n' roll. Folk was happening, he answered, and that was how he was going to make it; though it wasn't as good, it was definitely the coming thing.

Back in New York, things began to fall together. He was working with Hammond on a second album. He turned down an offer to play the Blue Angel nightclub and instead auditioned for "The Ed Sullivan Show." CBS would call back a year later, when, as Dylan feared, they would try to censor him. He also had contact with the Congress of Racial Equality (CORE), and

On the streets of Greenwich Village, 1963. (© 1977 Jim Marshall)

that acronym appealed to him far more than those represented by the jacketed and tied uptown men.

And as Dylan looked on the world, songs began to emerge from his pen with amazing rapidity. He still "borrowed" tunes, but the lyrics and performance were all Dylan's own, so it didn't and wouldn't matter much if "Bob Dylan's Dream" was based on "Lord Franklin," "Restless Farewell" was a reworked bluegrass tune called "Little Moses," or "Blowin' in the Wind" owed a huge debt to "No More Auction Block." He was doing what Woody had done before him and many others did before Woody—making music, and making a name for himself with songs that amazed the entire Village scene. Later on, that August day he walked downtown and changed his name legally to Bob Dylan, the transformation was complete, *all* the baby fat was finally gone.

The songs coming out of him now were protest songs. In January, 1962, he penned "The Ballad of Emmett Till" for CORE, and it was the best song he'd written, even though the melody was lifted from a Len Chandler tune. He seemed to be learning that Woody's way was fine, but he had to write about times happening, not times past, and soon any news was grist for his mill. Woody couldn't help him here, though he was the final idol. Through Guthrie he'd found his voice and discovered that "image" was often a separate, controlled reality. Dylan knew he had to do it on his own.

Late in February, *Bob Dylan* hit the record bins; it sold poorly that first year. Quickly he was dubbed "Hammond's Folly" in the intrigue-laden corridors of power at CBS. Some of the businessmen at Columbia were already trying to get him off the label, but with both Hammond and Johnny Cash firmly behind him, the contract remained secure. Hammond knew Bob was far past the traditional songs on his first album, and knew that the delightful interplay of harmonica, guitar and voice that Dylan used on others' songs would, when used on his own, new, topical material, convey the urgency, chaos, pessimism, doom and hope of a locomotive from Hibbing huffing its way to fame. Encouraged by the publication that same month of *Broadside,* a magazine devoted to the topical song, and his subsequent signing with M. Witmark & Sons, a music publishing firm, protest songs poured out of him.

Dylan's first triumph was The Newport Folk Festival of 1963. (© 1977 Jim Marshall)

In April, the struggle for civil rights resulted in a song he called "Blowin' in the Wind," written to lash out against the betrayal of American ideals through a conspiracy of silence. He was knocked out by the song, as were his friends. When it was published in the sixth *Broadside,* late in May, it began to appear as if the entire tradition of American folk and a whole new generation of Americans who could afford a conscience were guiding his pen. The songs were already there anyway, he said, they were just waiting for someone to pluck them from the air. Whether he was writing them out of belief or, as later charged, out of commercial instinct, the songs stood on their own, hitting chords that had never been played before. His trips back home were fewer and shorter as the excitement in the Village grew. His relationship with Suze was on the rocks, though with her almost gone he wrote intense love songs along with his topical political numbers.

The fame machine was cranking up in earnest now. In early fall, the prestigious folk song magazine *Sing Out!* featured him on its cover. On September 22, Dylan appeared with many of the other big names in folk at a hoot at Carnegie Hall. Among the songs he played were "A Hard Rain's A-Gonna Fall," an apocalyptic vision of nuclear holocaust, and "Talkin' John Birch Paranoid Blues," a biting satire of America's right wing, then both active and worth taking seriously. Other songs of the period included "Oxford Town," written about James Meredith's attempts to register at Ole Miss, "The Death of Emmett Till," and "Let Me Die in My Footsteps," an impassioned cry against the madness of fallout shelters, in which Dylan stated categorically that he would "not go down under the ground." Even as he stood with the other superstars of folk, it was becoming clear that Dylan dominated the world of the topical song.

In November, Dylan began recording his second album in earnest. Quoted as saying that every line of "Hard Rain" was a song he was afraid he'd never get to write, he continued living, writing, performing, and missing his woman with the passion of someone sure his time was short. America and Russia had come to the brink over Cuba in October. The other fellow blinked, but that was no proof that the brink had disappeared. "The cause" seemed that much more valid as the superpowers relaxed from their Cuban muscle flexing.

There was plenty of tension during this time. Problems arose between Grossman, John Court (Grossman's partner), and Hammond. Bob had recently switched publishers to Warner Brothers. Recording was temporarily put off when, in late December, an invitation came from BBC in England for Dylan to appear in a drama. A $1000 fee was the sweetener. On January 12,

Bob appeared in England in a television play called "Madhouse on Castle Street," playing the part of a hobo. He sang "Blowin' in the Wind" and "Swan on the River," a song that would never be heard again. His performance elicited mild response; the show was a bomb. But London wasn't a complete waste of time. He hooked up with Ric Von Schmidt and Richard Fariña and for several days after the telecast they all ran around London getting crazy and even recording an album at Dobell's, London's best folk music store. Blind Boy Grunt was again in attendance at this strange session.

Even though Suze moved in with Bob when he returned to the City, the tensions were still high between them, and he had tension enough to deal with now, more than ever before. As he returned to New York's streets to gather more material for his song-poems, Grossman's other acts, and most of the folk world, were realizing that the slight man was creating a new genre of beautiful, meaningful songs, *saying things* that had to be said. The tunes and production were subordinated to the all-important, rushing, spilling lyrics. His Town Hall concert on April 12, 1963, was a triumph, and people began to take the idea of Dylan as poet seriously, thanks to his program notes, "My Life in a Stolen Moment," and his encore reading of "Last Thoughts on Woody Guthrie."

The next step was the recording of *The Freewheelin' Bob Dylan*, marred slightly by Hammond's resigning as producer because of Grossman's power moves. Tom Wilson took over the album and produced the last four tunes: "North Country Girl," "Talking World War III Blues," "Bob Dylan's Dream," and "Masters of War." Originally they were not scheduled for that album but corporate foolishness at CBS forced their inclusion.

Dylan had been invited to appear on the Sullivan show in mid-May. Sullivan and his producer had both okayed "Talkin' John Birch Society Blues" for Bob to sing on the prestigious Sunday night variety show. However, at the dress rehearsal, Dylan was told he couldn't perform it by some official from CBS program practices. Bob split in a huff on learning CBS found the song libelous. CBS also deleted the song from the upcoming album. Though copies of the completed album had been circulated, it was ultimately re-released with the four Wilson-produced tracks added and "Birch," "Ramblin' Gamblin' Willie," "Rocks and Gravel," and "Let Me Die in My Footsteps" removed. With the album about to come out, Dylan left New York for some concerts and promotional appearances.

Freewheelin' sold astonishingly well from the moment of its release. By mid-May Bob was making more money than most of his contemporaries. Once Peter, Paul and Mary's version of "Blowin' in the Wind" was released, Bob was recognized as a major new talent. To Hammond, Dylan had lost something, his political strand was dying out. Or maybe it was the big money and Albert Grossman who'd turned Bob into a businessman. What mattered was that Columbia was planning to make him the world's greatest protest singer, and they snickered in their boardrooms as they learned how all the other companies were beating the Village for their own Dylan surrogates.

He played the first Folk Festival at Brandeis University May 10 and 11, 1963, then traveled to California for the first Monterey Folk Festival. Since both Pete Seeger and the Weavers were banned from appearing on ABC-TV's new show, *Hootenanny*, the young folksingers stayed away; thus festivals grew in importance.

Even more important, at Monterey, Dylan again met Joan Baez whom he'd previously criticized for her noninvolvement. Now Baez was saying that she felt it, but Bob could say it. After Monterey, Bob stayed in Carmel with Baez for several weeks. She invited him to tour with her that summer. A close relationship was developing between these two folk giants.

On July 6, Dylan appeared in Greenwood, Mississippi, at a voter registration rally with Pete Seeger, Theodore Bikel, and Josh White, and sang a new song, "Only a Pawn in Their Game," about the murder of civil rights leader Medgar Evers. That song, along with others he was now writing, revealed something special about Dylan, something that would soon lead him away from protest songs and that inner burning fire. Dylan was not protesting; rather he was seeing the world in a different way, from a different sensibility than had ever before provided the basis for such selfconscious art. A reporter, he still fit events into his own unique perspective, a perspective that would be seen as more important than the events themselves. He could only explain that he saw no difference between black and white so many times. He would attend few other "protest rallies."

Later in July, Dylan attended his first Newport Folk Festival, the gathering of folk's gods and goddesses. New deities were preparing to overthrow the old order at the annual rites. City talent—Dylan, 21, Phil Ochs, 22, Mark Spoelstra, 23, Len Chandler, 25, Tom Paxton, 25, and Peter La Farge, 32,

At a workshop. Joan Baez sits beside Dylan. (© 1977 Jim Marshall)

were dubbed Woody's Children by Pete Seeger. Peter, Paul and Mary's "Blowin'" single had sold 320,000 copies in its first eight days of release. These young kids from the city were giving folk music a new lease on life, and the audiences, whether old leftists or folklorists, were salivating at the chance to adopt them, call them their own.

Dylan played the first night and went down a smash. Offstage, he played with a bullwhip and again was called arrogant. Some old-timers were pissed off by the brash young prince. As fame moved closer, Dylan seemed to be pushing back, sensing for the first time that keeping his voice might be more important than becoming bigger than Elvis. It put him uptight already. Dylan was on the verge of discovering that there was validity in an entirely anti-political stance, but, for the time being, he was still a big-time protest singer, like Joan Baez, the "Queen of Folk."

Even with all the attention he was receiving, Dylan retained his sharp humor, and the barbs were not blunted by his acceptance by the folk world, which seemed far out to the rest of America, but was, in retrospect, as conservative as any society where everyone dressed alike.

As the weekend wore on, with excitement bubbling through the thousands who attended, Dylan played duets with Pete Seeger and Baez, made cryptic comments about his relationship to folk music, and at the final, all-important Sunday evening concert, was called back onstage to join Seeger, Baez, the Freedom Singers and Peter, Paul and Mary. They all sang "Blowin' in the Wind," and then they began "We Shall Overcome" and all the performers came onstage, linked hands and sang in a moment of transcendent togetherness. Dylan was approaching the eye of the hurricane, though, and the moments of transcendence were too often followed by moments of terror.

After Newport, Dylan joined Baez for her short Northeastern tour, ending up in Washington, D.C., for the March on Washington, where Martin Luther King, Jr., spoke of having a dream to the 200,000 demonstrators crowded in front of the Lincoln Memorial. Baez, Odetta, Peter, Paul and Mary, Mahalia Jackson, Bob Dylan, and more sang, as across the country people black and white hoped this outpouring of sentiment would change the world. Dylan's songs showed him far beyond such innocence.

In New York at Joan's Forest Hills Stadium concert, Dylan's guest appearance caused shock waves. He was being recognized now as a prodigal superstar. Stories of his relationship with Baez were constantly being told. The Crown Prince of Folk was about to become the King, they said, and he'd rightfully join Joan Baez, the Queen. Together, one assumed, they would bring conscience to America. Back in New York after a summer of approaching and encroaching stardom, Dylan faced his slovenly apartment. Suze was gone and he had to find a place to figure it all out.

Dylan quickly moved up to Grossman's Woodstock retreat, where he could sort out his options. The rustic environment, Albert's concern, and the need to keep working must have kept him from Edge City. He was annoyed at the treatment Hammond had been given, scared now that he had things to lose, unsure whom he could trust, so he turned his business concerns over to Grossman and associates and went more into himself. Everyone *did* want a piece of him. He was, after all, making thousands of dollars a month. In September he entered the studio with Wilson to record his third album. In October he headlined concerts in Philadelphia and at New York's prestigious Carnegie Hall. (His parents flew in just for this moment.) On *Billboard*'s October album charts, one of every six albums was folk.

Clowning at the Viking Hotel pool with Joan Baez, Newport, 1963. (© 1977 Jim Marshall)

With Suze at Newport. (© 1977 Jim Marshall)

22

But as he was being touted as "a moralist, a pamphleteer," he was writing the last of his protest songs, "Restless Farewell," which would close his third album with a goodbye wave to finger-pointing songs, and the liner notes for that album, "11 Outlined Epitaphs," spelled it all out.

November 22, 1963. Mid-afternoon in New York. Dylan watched as millions of dreams died with JFK. He was in the midst of a short college tour. The next night, he played a show to a filled house. Like most Americans he was numb and, perhaps, a little afraid.

Just three weeks later, the full effects of Kennedy's assassination on Dylan's fragile psyche became known when, at a dinner featuring such luminaries as James Baldwin, he received the Emergency Civil Liberties Committee's Tom Paine Award. Though he'd later deny any overreaction, the speech he delivered at the Hotel Americana that night betrayed his anger and confusion. Drinking and thinking about his relationship to the old leftists in the room,

Dylan got uptight and tried to walk out. Caught, he stepped reluctantly to the dais and began to speak.

Yes he said, he was proud to be young in a young world, but politics were trivial and people didn't have to join movements or march to prove they felt strongly about causes. He rambled on incoherently about Kennedy and Oswald, Kennedy's assassin, as the crowd booed and the chairman kicked him under the table. Then someone said his time was up and he took his award and fled into the night. Immediately after the incident he sent off a letter to the committee. No, he couldn't apologize for being himself, he just felt it was getting tiresome to hate so much. After you hate something to death you find out that it really wasn't worth the trouble since time's river keeps flowing, and you've gotta keep up with the current.

Dylan came into his own that night, the "crisis" defining his new stance. He would no longer apologize for being Bob Dylan.

At the conclusion of the Festival's last concert, Dylan joined Peter, Paul and Mary, Joan Baez, and The Freedom Singers for an emotional farewell. (© 1977 Jim Marshall)

4: Honesty outside the Law

CHANGES CAME TO the life of Bob Dylan in 1964. While Lyndon Johnson and Barry Goldwater collided with their conflicting visions of what made America great, Dylan was taking the voice and skills he'd molded and trained and turning them toward a new expression of the sounds inside his mind. There was a sudden burst of communication from Bob Dylan to the world; the message to the Emergency Civil Liberties Committee was just the tip of the iceberg. In December, *Hootenanny,* which had been publishing Dylan regularly, carried a poem in which he reiterated he would not let his music run his life. December also saw the release of Peter, Paul and Mary's new album, the classic *In the Wind,* with Dylan liner notes. It was a retrospective piece about his first winter in New York. He thought of the singers who were then around, playing at the Gaslight, and a show one night when the door was locked and no tourists intruded. The notes were wistful, nostalgic, ending with the thoughts of Peter, Paul and Mary's growth and the inexorable passing of time.

(© Diana Davies/Nancy Palmer Photo Agency, Inc.)

(Pictorial Parade)

Broadside contained Dylan's January communiqué, a rambling monologue on fame and the good fight. He described his feelings on becoming a personality. Occasionally he enjoyed it, but he still felt guilt and fear. In *his* world, every man would have an even shot. He described walking down the Bowery, giving money away and still feeling guilty for not having enough money to give. Someone told him he'd need the money one day, and he just thought it was useless. Too many people wanted too many things. He talked about love and the apartment he was moving out of and Pete Seeger singing "Guantanamera," his novel, and his plays. The ramble's a strange one, confusing, no doubt reflecting the state of the mind of the author.

By February, and his liner notes for *Joan Baez in Concert, Part 2,* Dylan was writing more about himself than before, using his own conscience rather than his political position as his standard, as he'd suggested in his *Broadside* rambling. He wrote about his discovery of the beauty in Baez's voice, but the story he told was far more reaching than that. It began in a railroad field near his aunt's house, where as a "frightened fox" and "demon child" he'd watch the locomotives go by, staining his hands green as he pulled grass from the

Onstage with Baez, Newport, 1964. (© *1977 Jim Marshall)*

field in excitement, a lonely child lost in himself. Later, walking alone in a friendless world, striking out in "phantom brawls" with symbols like the word "beautiful," he was a "saddened clown" in a self-made circus of the mind. Soon even his idols were shot down, but he continued to do battle with beauty, a rebel, "an arch criminal" who committed no crimes, but was locked nonetheless in another's prison.

Dylan came to New York where he found beauty in the filth of the city, embraced it and took its voice. Then he met a girl "on common ground,"

but could only hear the ugliness in her voice. He was what he termed a "scared poet" but Joan Baez was about to prove to him that he could still grow. He described a car ride during which she talked of the violence of her childhood. The stories of dogs being beaten to death brought his mind back to the boy who pulled up grass in a field. Maybe there was something in her voice, he thought, but guilt was all he felt. Then he described a night in Woodstock, when, at a painter's home, drunk on light red wine, in a resting mood, he listened to her sing and could not hear the ugliness, and Baez laughed with Dylan as the wall between them fell.

He discovered himself to be foolish for trying to dissect the sounds of nature. Beauty shouldn't be questioned by those who find answers anywhere but in themselves, Dylan says, standing up, pointing to himself, declaring that when spring comes he'll return to the field of his youth, wait for cars filled with iron ore, count the grass instead of killing it, and tell the engineer Joanie says hello as he speeds by, past the "rebel wild" who has learned not only who he is, but how not to hurt.

The fact that Dylan could write with such touching clarity about himself and his own feelings marked the end of a period of his own growth. Concurrent with that change, as poetess Patti Smith might say, a rhythm was generating across the oceans. It would bring a wave of relief to a battered America whose heroes—James Bond or JFK—had been proud, bursting with promise, ready for a fall; it would revive the optimism of the Kennedy years as, at the same time, it marked the difference between pre- and post-war generations and set the two in a course of opposition that would last a decade.

In February, preceded by a hit single and a press blitz of unheard-of proportions, the Beatles arrived in America. There they were, shaking it for freedom on "Ed Sullivan," larking in the Miami surf, clowning with another symbol just arrived on the scene, Cassius Clay, who was about to whup Sonny Liston with the same force that the English Invasion would whup Tin Pan Alley, creating the rock business and several other cultural immensities in their wake.

Dylan was traveling, on a college tour Grossman had booked with dates in Atlanta, Denver, San Francisco and L. A. With a holding company set up to support him, Dylan could buy a Ford station wagon, put bodyguards on the payroll, and take to the road. Already, his bodyguards were around constantly, to minimize the necessity of Bob's coming in contact with the real world that grew increasingly unreal around him. Drugs were then drifting into the realm of possibility of young, hip white kids. "I'm pro-chemistry," Dylan was quoted as saying. Few doubted that. Exotic potions and forbidden fruits are available to most pop stars. Most try them, whether once or all the time. For two-and-a-half years, they would be an integral part of Dylan's universe, if not his personal chemistry.

With his earnings reportedly reaching six figures, Dylan could afford to do whatever he wanted, and what he chose to do was drive from city to city, in order to touch "the people" and fill in some of the blanks in his understanding of America and himself.

Richard Fariña (who'd been divorced by his first wife, Carolyn Hester, met Joan Baez's sister Mimi, married her and returned to California), wrote about Dylan's Berkeley appearance and subsequent stay with Baez in Carmel for *Mademoiselle* that summer. "Catch him now," Fariña wrote of the mood on campus before the show. "Next week he might be mangled on a motorcycle."

At the show, he played "Pawn," "Emmett Till," "Masters of War," and "With God on Our Side." Critics in the audience were upset by the confidence of Dylan and Baez, while the two, Fariña wrote, felt mere ovations were "dubious reward for their efforts."

Fariña noted that when Dylan and Baez were alone, they never spoke of protest, preferring metaphor to megatons. When Baez had first heard Dylan's

Dylan and Mike Seeger at Newport, 1964. (© *1977 Jim Marshall)*

new/old songs, she'd discovered the words to fit her feelings. When Dylan arrived in Carmel that spring, he found Joan, Mimi, their mother and Fariña. They ate beef stew cooked by Mother Baez, talked of old friends, listened to Everly Brothers records and to Paul Clayton. One girl at the concert had wondered why Dylan had changed his name. Because, Fariña wrote, Dylan had "stepped so cleanly away from his antecedents and into the exhilarating world of creative action as to make the precise nature of an early history look insignificant." The next day, Dylan headed for Hollywood, where he stayed in the Thunderbird Motel, went to parties and shows. He returned to New York in mid-March.

Meanwhile his reputation had been growing, as had the swirls of controversy that, once arrived, would never leave any critical discussion of his work. A graffitied subway ad in New York's 116th Street station read, "Bob Dylan doesn't know his ethnic musicology." Bobby Darin and Chubby Checker released folk albums. A letter to *Sing Out!* called Dylan "a so-called singer who never ceases to irritate," though a review of his third album in the next issue stated emphatically that with his minor chording, conscious poetry, eerie quality and deep insight, Dylan had come "entirely into his own."

The more Bob came into his own, the less common ground he seemed to

Dylan with the crowd at Newport, 1964. (© 1977 Jim Marshall)

share with others. The protective tricks he'd learned to deal with fans, groupies and leeches were occasionally turned on friends as well. Some felt his defensive posturing in intellectual company came out of his positive *feeling* orientation rather than from a negative inclination to intellect. Fame was pushing him. Sometimes he lost control, schizzing into the dark when Suze finally left him. Dylan's dependence on Bob Neuwirth, a Cambridge/Berkeley folk nomad, coincidentally grew. Neuwirth, himself described as egotistical, secretive, a catalyst, seemed to many to be pushing Bob into the role of hipster hero, giving him the room and the attitude to develop the pose.

Dylan was in a fragile state of mind, and though the *Life* magazine story that ran on him that spring still treated him as a protest singer, some of his comments heralded the coming of a "new" Bob Dylan. "My records are selling and I'm making money," he said, "but it makes me think I'm not doin' right. Man, I'm goin' through a weird time." He found some respite in music, playing piano as Bob Landy on an album called *The Blues Project* and harp as Tedham Porterhouse on one cut of a Jack Elliott album, but the changes he was going through still reigned supreme. "I don't want to write *for* people anymore. . . . I want to write from inside me." He was being pushed to produce material for a new album, and he had a tour of England planned. Not much time to think.

And Rock was *back;* it was Dylan's first love, and in May 1964, he left New York for its newest home, the center of the storm, England, which was swinging so hard the pendulum couldn't keep up. At Royal Festival Hall in London, he introduced his reform school song, "The Walls of Red Wing" as his "school song." He continued to rebel (if not rock and roll) in his May 23 interview with *Melody Maker* when he said, "One thing I know is that you can't please everybody. . . . I get put down a lot but I dig it when they slam me for some odd reason. . . . I don't think anything you plan *ever* turns out the way you plan."

For example, who could have guessed that the Beatles, the Rolling Stones, and the Animals would all turn out to be as much Dylan's fans as he was theirs. According to a 1977 article by Peter Stafford and Bruce Eisner in *High Times,* Allen Ginsberg recalled he and Dylan were both turned on to marijuana for the first time by *New York Post* rock columnist Al Aronowitz. "The Beatles were turned on by Dylan when their planes once crossed at JFK airport. He asked whether they wanted to turn on and they were hesitant. Finally Ringo said he'd try it. They went behind a hangar, and after returning to the others, Ringo was asked what he thought of it. He was smiling so much the others decided to try it too."

Backstage at Newport, 1964.
(© 1977 Jim Marshall)

The British pop groups were, in fact, schooled in the same musical heritage as Dylan, infatuated with the Black music of Chicago, Memphis, and the Delta, interested in giving pop music back its teeth, not in regurgitating the pap of the early Sixties. It was an invitation Dylan could hardly resist. He'd turned to folk because it was what was happening; now Murray the K was screaming about what was happening, and it wasn't acoustic guitars with high clear sopranos.

Much as Dylan believed in the causes he was singing about, and much as his newly found audience believed with him, folk was not his form. Protest was not the sound of his voice. Rock was the fitting musical form for an insane world, and its cries were the cries of those insane enough to live in it. Chemicals alone cannot explain the outsider experience of the young people

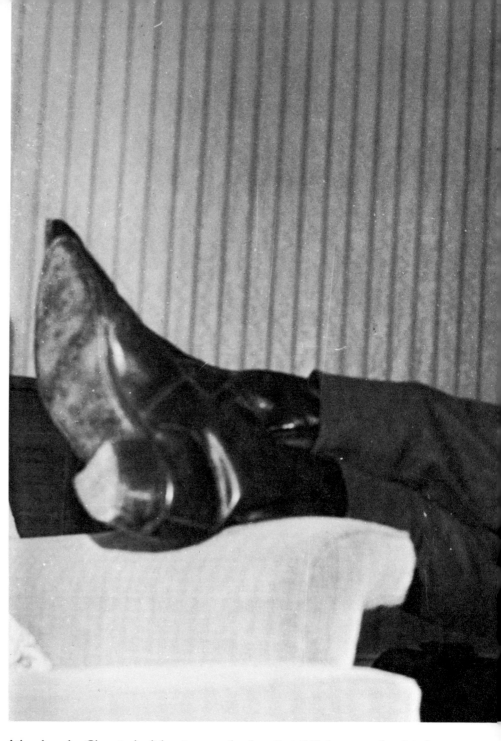

Dylan relaxes in Sheffield, England, April 1965. *(Photo Trends)*

of the decade. Chemicals did not cause the fear that if Dylan stayed political he might be killed. His world view was growing transcendent and he was being impelled away from political overtness. The entire world was becoming a shade of gray. Now in a state of constant artistic motion, he was set to make the move and take the giant risk implicit in the abandonment of the topical song. He couldn't move into rock yet, but he could write rock songs. Back in the studio with Tom Wilson, rushing an album for the CBS sales convention and spending the rest of his time upstate, Dylan had made the commitment to shed one role and seek whatever new one came along.

As he made the move, he *was* leaving a lot of people behind, people who would ultimately fend for themselves quite well. *Times* had only been released in January, and its songs of anger and rage were just beginning to

motivate people. A year later, protest, Vietnam, Peace Parades, little blue buttons with white and black interlocking hands would be the rage. Fifth Avenue in New York would be the scene of some of the greatest confrontations America had witnessed since the Civil War. The Great Society was a ripoff, and in Dylan's rage, young people saw the mirror image of their own frustration. "We Shall Overcome" became their anthem. Each year, as the babies who boomed crossed the line into majority, more and more would find their way to the streets to echo Dylan and wait for the hour when the ship would come in. For Bob, it was time to pick up the threads of "One Too Many Mornings," "North Country Blues," "Boots of Spanish Leather," and the amazing "Lay Down Your Weary Tune," and forge them a poetry all his own.

Playing electric, Dylan was set free. *(Photo Trends)*

That summer, Bob put the finishing touches on a new album, *Another Side of Bob Dylan,* and spent most of his time commuting between Columbia Studios in New York and Albert Grossman's palatial house in Woodstock (where Grossman provided stability and a buffer against the outside world). It was an interesting departure and new direction. As Richard Fariña said in the liner notes for his own album *Celebrations for a Grey Day,* recorded at approximately the same period, "Time, tide, and the accident of what the statisticians call birth have conspired to provide us with a tradition barely ours and hardly its own. Music, if it has a mind to, can sing about things like that, and maybe set one or two of them straight, yes?" "Chimes of Freedom," the most affecting song on this new disc, was singing about such things, at the same time that Dylan was circumscribing the world of his peers with a new one all his own. In the complex language he was beginning to use, tying the fragmentary images of a song like "Hard Rain" into the cohesive whole of

"Chimes," Dylan was beginning to create the language that would speak for everyone.

"Motorpsycho Nightmare," Dylan's interpretation of Hitchcock's *Psycho*, followed. The song, along with "I Don't Believe You" (which would be updated electronically a few years later), heralded the coming change in instrumentation by using rock form, even though the songs were recorded with nothing but Dylan's voice, guitar and harmonica. These songs begged for electricity. Soon Dylan would provide it. In the space of a few days he recorded the whole of his album. The last song, "My Back Pages," was an attack on the life he'd been leading for the past year. Much of his anger was aimed within, as he decried his own use of ideas as maps, his romance with black and white, the notions of "corpse evangelists" and "self-ordained professors." "I was so sure," he wrote, "I became that which I railed against, secure in a fantasy world of good and bad." But the world was not set up that way and when he sang that he "was so much older then" but "younger than that now," Dylan made his feelings clear.

When *Another Side* appeared, the gauntlet was down for the folkies. "Black Crow Blues" marked Dylan's piano debut. The "No, no, no" refrain of "It Ain't Me, Babe" echoed the "Yeah, Yeah, Yeah's" of the Beatles' "She Loves You," and George Harrison had even been quoted as approving of Dylan: "I like his whole attitude," Beatle George said, anticipating the way a whole new audience would feel about Dylan. "The way he dresses, the way he doesn't give a damn, the way he sings discords and plays discords. The way he sends up everything."

In Israel, "Blowin' in the Wind" was finally a hit. In England, *Freewheelin'* was voted best folk album of 1964 and Bob, "best new talent." New Dylans were appearing often enough to earn a Dubious Achievement Award from *Esquire*. In June, he quietly attended his brother David's high school graduation in Hibbing. In July, he played the '64 Newport Festival, an overcrowded affair where intimacy was a wistful memory. There Dylan was much more the citified Midwestern boy than the Prince of Protest. The music he played expressed symbolically the words he'd written for the back of *Another Side,* words crammed in tiny print on the back of the album, headed "Some other kinds of songs . . . ."

Sing Out!'s Irwin Silber understood what Dylan was trying to say, and that fall, post-Newport, post-*Another Side,* he made his feelings known in an open letter. Worried about Dylan's new "bag," concerned that he'd lost contact with reality through the excess baggage of fame, Silber wrote that the last time he'd seen Dylan he "cried a little inside . . . for that awful potential for self-destruction which lies in all of us." Silber found the new songs too personal, maudlin and cruel, private jokes, undemocratic. He ended with a warning:

"The American Success Machinery chews up geniuses at a rate of one a day and still hungers for more. Unable to produce real art on its own, the Establishment breeds creativity in protest. . . . And then, through notoriety, fast money and status, it makes it almost impossible for the artist to function and grow."

Almost.

In the next issue of *Sing Out!,* the letter columns were full of the Dylan problem. The magazine's review of *Another Side,* contained in that issue, was waffling, saying the album raised questions which couldn't be answered, ending, "Many breezes are blowing in the wind." To one letter writer, Dylan had lost touch with his audience. To another, he'd found it. "What do culturally unspoiled kids on the street corners in the city slum sing?" Geoffrey Brown asked. "Rock and roll."

In Berkeley, the Free Speech Movement was exploding. On the record charts, British Pop was dominant. Nineteen sixty-four was the year of the Englishmen. Countless Bob Dylan copies sat around the Village waiting for Bob's next move since now each of his appearances was an *event*. In August he was with Baez in Forest Hills, singing "With God on Our Side," "It Ain't Me, Babe," and "Mama, You Been on My Mind." The first was one of his most sublime protest songs. The last, sung first, was a love song, possibly to Baez. The song in the middle was the gauntlet Dylan was throwing down to the world that summer and fall. Not a recounting of, or a reaction to the death of his affair with Suze (like "All I Really Want to Do," "Black Crow Blues," "I Don't Believe You (She Acts Like We Never Have Met)," or "Ballad in Plain D," the most obvious song to Suze), "It Ain't Me Babe," soon to be a hit by the Turtles, was Dylan's declaration of his freedom to ramble, from folk, from Baez, from the little things or the big things—like the expectations of the audience. He was his own man, and he'd damn well pursue his own course. Follow at your own risk, he warned.

"It's Halloween and I've got my Bob Dylan mask on," Bob said at his October 31, 1964, concert at New York's Philharmonic Hall. And there he was, to the folkies' dismay, gone the funky old Gibson, replaced by an expensive new instrument. But he was hot, getting hotter; criticism rolled off him as he debuted in his new style, songs like "Gates of Eden," "It's All Right Ma (I'm Only Bleedin')," "Mr Tambourine Man," and "If You Gotta Go, Go Now," an outtake from *Another Side*.

Dylan was now running on a very special kind of energy. At times it seemed he'd live out Fariña's and Silber's worst predictions, tearing around Woodstock and New York City on his big Triumph motorcycle. There was a strange contrast there. The wild boy on a powerful machine he couldn't control. The wild boy writing words the likes of which only experience, teachers tell us, can grant.

Michael Gray, teacher of English literature and author of the only critical work on Dylan's songs, called "Gates of Eden" Blakeian, referring to Dylan's opposing images, "of material wealth and spiritual; of earthly reality and the imaginatively real; of the body and the soul of false gods and true vision; of self-gratification and salvation; of mortal ambitions and the celestial city; of sins and forgiveness; of evil and good," but even such highly admirable literary analysis could not equal the visceral shock of hearing such a song for the first time, with Dylan's swirling guitar figures nearly overwhelmed by the tortured vocal, and knowing that right there was a confused and confusing evocation of just what the listener was feeling.

Dylan was twenty-three years old, and yet he seemed to have lived it all, with "it" defined as the exclusive experience of anyone who called himself young in 1964. That let out Dean Rusk and Lyndon J. and McGeorge Bundy and Governor Wallace, the *New York Times,* gray-flanneled dwarves and other mistakes of history. An old person who was young? Dylan suggested "Fidel Castro and his beard."

In Woodstock, Albert Grossman's wife Sally had introduced Bob to a friend

of hers, Sara Lowndes, a model with a daughter. She'd worked as a Playboy Bunny and lived in the Chelsea Hotel in New York. Sometime between late 1964 and mid-'65, Dylan also took an apartment in the Chelsea. It's said he liked Sara because she didn't ask a lot of questions. She was Zen-like, never argued or judged or looked too far for too much.

Woodstock was Dylan's spiritual home, but by late 1964 it was drawing a certain type of hip, young person. Not necessarily musicians, but close enough—music business types would be closer. The Woodstock Music and Art Fair of 1969 drew in some part on the mystique Dylan had created about the place. Where else would the spirit of a generation come together for three days of peace and love?

Up in Woodstock though, Dylan was as funky as ever. He still had the Ford station wagon, now a little beat-up, and still used it. He stayed in seedy motel rooms while on the road, a lingering example of his fear of attracting attention. He still wore boots and jeans, though dark shirts were added to his performing wardrobe. Over them he wore a close copy of the stained suede jacket he'd had since he hit New York. He was a freak before freakiness became the rage in America.

This freakishness was evident in the fragments of the various literary projects Dylan had been trying—plays, novels, stories, and his autobiography, which he'd first alluded to publicly in 1963 when he told an interviewer in Chicago that he was writing a book "about my first week in New York." Though he seemed to know it lacked focus and was thus not as strong as his songs, he was determined to finish a prose piece, and worked on it with the same single-minded precision he'd give each aspect of his career. Bob Markel, a senior editor at the Macmillan Company, was approached by Grossman's office to publish Dylan's work.

"I met Albert Grossman before I met Bob Dylan," Markel recalled, "sometime in the mid-Sixties. Bob was just beginning to make an impression as a singer and writer. Albert explained to me that he thought Dylan was a very hot property who might want to do a book one day, and that if I were interested, we might be able to work out a contract for a book." Dylan said later that "contracts came in the mail," and he apparently signed one without much thought. Markel remembered the contract's originally being drawn up for a book of photographs of Hollywood life and culture by Barry Feinstein (then married to Mary Travers of Peter, Paul and Mary), with a text by Dylan.

"Around that time, we did sign a contract with Bob Dylan, so it very well might have arrived in the mail," Markel continued. "We gave him an advance for an untitled book of writings. I had not met him. The idea was, the publisher was taking a risk on a young, untested potential phenomenon. In time we'd figure out a book, but it was worth having a contract. He was uncertain what the book would be. We were hoping to get something, and by having his name on a contract, we'd be doing something.

"Macmillan had one of the principal poetry programs of those days. It had a long history of publishing major American poets. The editor who handled the poetry, a poet in his own right, came to me and said he'd heard that we'd signed a book of blank verse by Dylan, to be published as poetry. He said that if it was listed as poetry when it appeared in the catalog, he would resign, and I reassured him that he wouldn't have to do that.

"I believe our first meeting took place in the great big marvelous old downtown Macmillan offices. It was probably the winter of 1964. When I spoke to Bob on the telephone he asked that the meeting take place after dark as he felt he couldn't travel in broad daylight. He was driving a motorcycle around New York in those days. I agreed to a 5:30 meeting so he wouldn't be followed by a mob. He came in the company of Joan Baez. They arrived and the receptionist at the bottom of the immense marble stairway prevented them from coming upstairs.

"I had to come down and identify them on the grounds that in her view they were disorderly persons. I reassured the ancient receptionist that they were legit. She was quite concerned that I'd let such disreputable types into the building. They were dressed very much in the fashion of the times, unkempt in the eyes of a seventy-year-old Irishwoman used to authors dressed in tweed and smoking pipes. They looked as though they couldn't possibly have anything to do with a proper publisher.

"There was no book at the time. Bob said he was fooling around with some material. At a later meeting, also with Baez, they were both drinking tea, and there was material, because we were discussing titles. The first title I ever saw on it was *Side One*.

"Joan, sipping her tea, looked up and asked if I'd given any thought to calling it *Fuck You*. And I, sipping my tea as well, said we'd thought of that already and rejected it, whereupon she indicated that to be a perfectly sensible answer to a sensible question, and proceeded to the next discussion.

"The material at that point was hazy, sketchy. The poetry editor called it 'inaccessible.' The symbolism was not easily understood, but on the other hand, it was earthy, filled with obscure but marvelous imagery. It had life, excitement, a real pulse. It was worth more than our poetry editor expected. I felt it had a lot of value and was very different from Dylan's output till then. It was not a book. It was the beginnings of what became *Tarantula*.

"Later, more material arrived, we met, and my suggestions were generally met with an agreeable nod. He seemed on occasion to be distant, distracted, but wherever we met he seemed to get involved by whatever was going on around him. Albert's offices then were like Grand Central Station on July 3." Work continued on *Side One,* as it did on Dylan's recording career, soon to enter obviously a distinct new phase.

America was about to take a long hard ride on an unleashed electric current. The Village especially was charged. Musically, everything was being thrown against the wall, and large amounts were sticking. The earliest moments in the lives of bands like the Blues Project, with Danny Kalb and Al Kooper, the Butterfield Blues Band, and the Fugs, with Allen Ginsberg, Gregory Corso, Tuli Kupferberg and Ed Sanders pitching in, were happening. In the relative wilds of Los Angeles, two ex-folkies, David Crosby and Jim McGuinn (who'd previously played the Playhouse in New York, advertised as "Jim McGuinn—Beatle Impressions") were forming the Byrds. They would go on to hear a demonstration tape of "Mr. Tambourine Man" and record it with electric backing, eliciting a "fucking wild!" from the tune's author. The Byrds, signed by Hammond after Bob made it big, recorded several Dylan songs on an early album.

"The Byrds," John Hammond said, "whom we signed after Bobby made it, recorded an album mostly of Dylan's tunes and I think that the sound of the Byrds doing his material really turned him on very much. I would suspect that had a lot to do with Bobby changing." There was also a "tremendous acceptance of Dylan's material among rock groups. . . . It made perfect sense: anything that would communicate with more people, with more kids, made sense."

In January 1965, Dylan entered Columbia studios with Tom Wilson producing to record *Bringing It All Back Home,* a landmark album with lyrics from Dylan's inner psyche backed by funky rock and roll. Dylan arrived at the studio with eighteen new songs, most written in an intense two-week period. Wilson himself chose all the musicians except Bruce Langhorn, a guitarist Bob wanted. The band was musically impeccable and spontaneous. Most of the songs were recorded in under five takes, as Dylan orchestrated tempos and solos, working with Wilson to perfect the new sound. People filled the studio, adding ideas and talent, sandwiches and wine. Bob worked with each musician individually, sure of what he wanted, glad to have good advice. When a take was far from right, he'd move into the next song so as not to break the rhythm. One moment on the record told a great deal about the atmosphere in the studio, when, at the beginning of "Bob Dylan's 115th Dream," the song opened on acoustic guitar, and the rest of the musicians missed their cue to come in. When Dylan realized they hadn't picked up, he cracked up and the whole studio did too. Finally he said, "Start it again, fellas," and the tape rolled on. Afterward, Dylan insisted the mistake stay on the album.

On the next-to-last day of recording, Dylan laid down three of the four solo tracks that would comprise the second side of the disk, playing "Mr. Tambourine Man," "Gates of Eden," and "It's All Right Ma (I'm Only Bleedin')" straight through without a playback. He told the engineers he didn't want to play the songs more than once. What you hear is what they got. The final addition to the accoustic side, "It's All Over Now, Baby Blue," was among the first of Dylan's songs to undergo a great deal of interpretation, as critics (self-ordained professors?) claimed the song was strong commentary on American military interventions around the world and America's crumbling domestic social structure. Others claimed it was a goodbye to a woman, a precursor of "Like a Rolling Stone," but the symbolism of this song—as well as "It's All Right Ma" (which would still be current in 1969 when it was included in the soundtrack for the film *Easy Rider*), "Gates of Eden," and the supposedly drug-infested "Mr. Tambourine Man"—was general to the experience of vast numbers of young people in America; general enough, in fact, that it would remain current for years, as Dylan picked up more and more listeners.

"Subterranean Homesick Blues," filled with staccato advice, had a line for everyone, from the yet-to-be-born Weathermen who'd take their name from the song to every drug freak who'd ever own a stereo, and who, in the first verse, heard the entire tale of going out to cop: from Johnny who mixed the medicine to the buyer waiting for his man, the guy in the trench coat wanting a payoff and the man who wants more money than you got. "Look out, kid" indeed! In the final verse, one of Dylan's many indictments of the American Dream ended the tune with a bang. Play by the rules and you still end up a fool, Dylan wrote. Instead, live underground, light candles, chew gum and don't be a bum.

With electric guitars behind it, the song was a scream and a subtle, strong invitation. Rock 'n' roll was an updating of Peter Pan, the cry of eternal youth. America, in a side-effect of technology, had given its children the leisure of electronic life, with radios, TVs, tape machines, amps with echo and reverb, and the greatest icon of all, the electric guitar. Woody's music box killed fascists. With an electric guitar, you could rule the world, or at least make it notice you long enough to say, "Shut up!"

London Airport: "It's never been like this before." *(Photo Trends)*

"Outlaw Blues" was just what it promised to be, a joyful celebration of Dylan's new stance and new freedom; "On the Road" was a racing, hilarious description of same.

The love songs on the album were of a new sort, too. "She Belongs to Me" and "Love Minus Zero/No Limit" were the most mature representations he'd yet concocted of the half-real/half-dreamed woman a Dylan would love, an untouched and untouchable woman, who could think of love as no more than a four-letter word, casting spells on her prey, collecting men like antiques, but still a broken-winged raven on a cold, stormy night.

Dylan wrote that "They" would kill him if they knew what he was thinking in "It's All Right Ma." He set down there a number of the presumptions from which he wrote and would write for the rest of the time he'd spend at the hurricane center of the rock world. First, there was without question a "They" out there, and regardless of how They did it, They'd do it to you if

They got the chance. Sometimes, insidiously, They and you were the same. Second, Dylan's thoughts, and by extension the thoughts of his listeners, were different, dangerous, possibly revolutionary in their very nature. They were thoughts based on a clearly different perceptual process, and a far wider range of possibility. Thoughts that met no standards, and would not, in fact, consider the existence of standards. Thoughts that would bring down the wrath of the gods if revealed to Them. Romantic thoughts. *Dangerous* thoughts.

Dylan was on the verge of the most important move in his career and he seemed to sense it. In March, *Bringing It All Back Home* was released, bringing rock and roll back home to the country that had invented it and Bob Dylan back to his roots. It was met with derision from the folk establishment. That was no surprise. "Only a completely non-critical audience, nourished on the watery pap of pop music, could have fallen for such 10th-rate drivel," wrote Ewan MacColl, a distinguished folk historian, in the same symposium that proposed Phil Ochs as the "new" Dylan. Irwin Silber worried that it was "a freak and a parody of his own best self," the ravings of an unchained, nihilistic revolutionary as opposed to the "uncompromising anger and love of the poet." The same issue of *Sing Out!* reported Dylan with three albums in the British Top 10 and two others bubbling just beneath it. "Discreet full-page ads in trade papers tell you he is bigger in London than Big Ben," *Sing Out!* said in a tone best described as peeved. While plans were laid for an extensive English tour, Dylan took to the road with Baez to support the album and a single, "Subterranean Homesick Blues," released the first week of April for an eight-week stay on *Billboard*'s Top 100 chart, where it would peak at #39. It would ultimately become his first gold record.

Dylan contemplating the castle of Hamlet at Elsinore. *(UPI)*

Most reports agree that Dylan and Baez's non-professional relationship was in the midst of a year-long peak at the album's release. It had begun with Baez the star and Dylan the aspirant; it ended with Dylan's far surpassing Baez's strong professional position. As they toured together, sharing the spotlight in the spring of 1965, Dylan would enjoy it, though there must have been tension as Bob became a Certified Teen Idol. Some of Dylan's hip entourage no doubt cracked wise about Joan's naive involvement in the Institute for the Study of Nonviolence, then being challenged by sentiments like "Burn Baby Burn," leaking from Northern ghettos set to smoke. By the end of the tour the tension was thick enough to touch, they didn't sing together again until the Rolling Thunder Tour over a decade later.

The conflict between old Dylan and new was great enough that a Canadian weekly scandal tabloid, *The Confidential Flash,* bannered a page-three headline about the "Troubled Troubadors." "Dylan appears to have turned his back on any sort of personal improvement or development. . . . Dylan has gone from 'hobo camp' to 'high camp' in three short years."

On May 15, 1965, the Byrds' single "Mr. Tambourine Man" hit the charts for the beginning of a run that would last till the end of August. Pop stations told their listeners all about the "new" songwriting talent, Bob Dylan. Columbia Records promptly dubbed it all a teenage sound, though Dylan said of the Byrds, "They create a vision when they sing." Excitement was building fast by May when Dylan left for England with Joan Baez, Albert Grossman, and a cinema verité film crew led by D. A. Pennebaker.

Dylan was a bigger star there than he was in America; "Subterranean

Homesick Blues" was an award-winning hit. Two concerts planned for Albert Hall in London sold out within four hours of the tickets' going on sale. The Beatles and Donovan, a British "new Dylan," were certified Dylan groupies. Two shows were scheduled for broadcast over BBC. The *Daily Telegraph* called him the world's most important folksinger. He arrived at the airport carrying a giant industrial light bulb—he always carried a light bulb, he said, in fact he plugged it into his socket and his house exploded—har har. Within days he was decked out in the fashion of Britain 1965: high heels, Carnaby Street flowered shirts, a twenty-inch gray top hat, and pegged pants.

Later Dylan would denounce that documentary, *Don't Look Back,* but it endures as a record of his last acoustic tour, his last frustrating days as a folksinger. His attempts to break the pattern are the obvious high points of the film, though his acoustic performance belies his claimed lack of interest. The movie opens with Dylan in an alley, holding large signs with the lyrics from "Subterranean Homesick Blues," tossing them down as the song plays. His arrival with light bulb is next and then Dylan parries two reporters, calling himself delightful when they accuse him of being angry, insisting he'd glanced through the Bible but never read it. At a CBS press reception, Dylan refuses an award for *Freewheelin.'* "Tell them to give it to Donovan," he jokes. "Donovan . . . he's our target for tomorrow."

Later on in the film, when a young girl backstage tells Dylan she doesn't like his new single, he deadpans, "I have to give some work to my friends." But "The Times They Are A-Changin' " was a hit in England then, and Dylan was still being forced to appear as a folksinger. When a young rock band comes to meet him backstage after his show in Leicester, telling him they play his songs to a rock beat, but have trouble getting crowds to listen, Dylan tells them, "I'm not going to try to get anybody to listen."

A few scenes later, Dylan and Baez sit in a London hotel, singing old songs together, as Bobby Neuwirth listens. Bob taunts Baez, driving her from the room. (She'd say later that when she walked out that door, she left for France to visit her parents.) His treatment of a young science student interviewing him in the next scene was both an indication of his annoyance at being asked to solve the problems of the world, and his petulance, as he twists the young man around his finger, ripping into him, then telling him, "You don't know when you're liked," growing nearly humble when the interviewer is replaced by a High Sheriff's lady, come to tell him his songs are wonderful and he is a good example to youth. She invites him to her mansion, and leaves with, "Why, he's charming!"

Bob is not charming in the next scene, a party with Donovan in his hotel room, where he calls a drunk on the carpet, showing the fabled fangs. Still, when Donovan shows up to meet Dylan, they trade songs freely, with Dylan singing a few verses of "It's All Over Now, Baby Blue" for the Englishman.

Dylan's interview with an English *Time* magazine correspondent is the high point of the film, as he launches a diatribe without letting the man ask a question.

Reflecting on that night's concert, he tells the man, "It's going to happen fast . . . you're not going to get it all. . . . I won't be able to talk to you afterwards. . . . I got nothing to say about these things I write, I mean, I just write them. . . . I've never been in *Time* magazine and yet this hall's filled twice. . . . I'm not gonna read any of these magazines, I mean, 'cause they just got too much to lose by printing the truth. . . . I know more about what you do and you don't even have to ask me how or why or anything, just by

looking, you know, than you'll ever know about me, ever. . . . I could tell you I'm not a folksinger and explain to you why, but you wouldn't really understand. . . . I'm saying that you're going to die. . . . and how seriously you take yourself, you decide for yourself . . . and I'm just as good a singer as Caruso . . . a good singer, have to listen closely, but I hit all those notes and I can hold my breath three times as long if I want to."

At the Albert Hall concert, Dylan went over a smash, closing with "It's All Right, Ma (I'm Only Bleedin') Ho Ho Ho" and "Gates of Eden," waiting for the encore call with Neuwirth.

"Actually, applause is kind of bullshit," Dylan told Bobby. After the obligatory laugh, Neuwirth came back, "Wouldn't that be something else, though, if they just sat there and waited?"

At the end of the tour, Dylan and Grossman exercised a star's prerogative and flew to another country for a meal, returning with Dylan sick as a dog. Baez flew back from France, but was not welcomed. Sara was on or near the scene. Bob spent three days in the hospital, then flew home, frustrated—he'd rather do rock.

"Like a Rolling Stone," the song that would catapult Dylan into the arena of international stardom, was recorded at Columbia's Studio A on June 15, 1965. It was the last time Tom Wilson produced Dylan. The song was cut live in only a few takes, with Michael Bloomfield on guitar, Al Kooper on organ, and, possibly, Paul Griffin on piano. He used these same people the following day when he recorded "Tombstone Blues" and "Queen Jane Approximately" for his next album.

For Dylan there was an eerie kind of inevitability about writing "Rolling Stone," which began as a ten-page document of hatred and revenge. He

Poet Gerard Malanga joins Bob at Andy Warhol's Factory in New York City. *(From* The Secret Diaries, *a film by Gerard Malanga)*

never thought of it as a song until he caught the refrain, "How does it feel," when he was noodling around on the piano. It was like swimming in lava, being adrift, having nothing but yourself to hang onto in a world full of scroungers, mystery tramps, jugglers, and clowns, where you're stripped down to nothing and end up with nothing to lose. What's it like facing the void? Dylan cried the question out, and the song, his answer, would be his greatest triumph, rising to #2 on the *Billboard* charts, #1 in towns across America, and then around the world. If you didn't want us to think, Dylan's song said, you shouldn't have given us library cards.

"We listened to the Beatles to have fun," one observer noted, "but we listened to Dylan when we wanted to think." Bob Dylan was no longer the Prince of Protest. He'd been discovered by a whole new audience that overwhelmed his old one and their cries of "Traitor." Now he was the Poet of Pop, rock's prophet, the great white wonder. The protest songs, he was saying, were written within a small circle, where outsiders "could think something was happening which wasn't happening."

"If they can't understand green clocks, wet chairs, purple lamps or hostile statues," Dylan told the *Times'* Robert Shelton, "They're missing something. . . . My stuff is *me*, what seems to be happening in the songs is really happening."

Rationales for resentment would be obvious from the 1965 Newport Folk Festival and Forest Hills Stadium shows, where Dylan publicly unveiled his new sound for the first time. Dylan's Sunday, July 25th, appearance at the all-new improved Newport fest (on a larger site) scandalized many of the collegiate Village types in the crowd, who should have been forewarned by "Off the Top of My Head," some lines of Dylan's that appeared in the festival program. Its characters were Horseman and Photochick, who wears a Hoover button in her mouth, Prez, who wants the sound of the kazoos in his factory cut to "a higher pitch, perhaps like a girl screaming," his secretary Miss Flunk, and Tattler the errand boy, who tells Prez, "The dykes have broken down. They're beating everybody up and putting them in the closets." The piece cuts back to Horseman and Photochick, who've chopped down a pole, sprawled on the grass, and commented on an advertisement that wasn't there before, warning against cigars or, perhaps, advertising race car drivers smoking kazoos. "Meanwhile, back at the Newport Folk Festival . . ." Dylan concluded.

Early in the weekend, Dylan jammed with the Paul Butterfield Blues band, who were appearing at the festival for the first time. As Al Kooper remembered, "Rolling Stone" had been released that week and was "blasting out of every transistor radio smuggled onto the festival grounds, and Dylan wanted to make the penetration blatant." Mike Bloomfield, guitarist for Butterfield, brought along drummer Sam Lay, bassist Jerome Arnold, and pianist Barry Goldberg, and joined Dylan and Kooper that night for a rehearsal until dawn in a mansion on the Newport cliffs. Dylan was introduced Sunday night by Peter Yarrow. He was in his Carnaby Street best— leather jacket, black pants, polka-dot shirt, pointy high-heeled boots—and carried a solid-body electric guitar.

They opened the set with a raw "Maggie's Farm." The audience began to boo almost immediately. Two versions of the incident are generally told. One, propagated by *Sing Out!*, had Dylan playing two more songs, "It Takes a Lot to Laugh, It Takes a Train to Cry" and "Like a Rolling Stone," to increasing boos and cries that he should get rid of the electric guitar. After "Stone" he stormed from the stage, allegedly with tears in his eyes, to return after Yarrow tried to convince the audience to clap, saying, "Bob s gone to get his acoustic guitar," as George Wein, head of the festival, asked Yarrow in disbelief, "Is he coming back?" Everyone was sad, *Sing Out!* claimed, even Pete Seeger, who also had tears in his eyes over Dylan's betrayal of the purity of folk.

But Dylan, Kooper, and others take issue with that story. Ric Von Schmidt recalled that the yells began because Dylan's voice was overwhelmed by the instruments, and the first cries were simply for more volume on the vocal, with hecklers then gaining the guts to do what hecklers do. According to Kooper, by the time the band reached "Stone" they were sailing, and finished, having only planned three electric songs. Dylan, he said, was "satisfied" and the crowd was yelling for more. Dylan told Yarrow they'd only rehearsed three songs and Yarrow told him to play alone, which he did.

He came back on his acoustic, played a pointed "It's All Over Now, Baby Blue," responded to requests for "Mr. Tambourine Man" with "All right people, I'll sing that for ya," and left the stage with controversy and a carload of publicity swirling about his curly-haired, sunglassed head. "They can boo 'til the end of time," he said later. "I know that the music is real, more real than the boos."

Writers in *Sing Out!* and the *Village Voice* attacked Dylan's betrayal. The "fan mail" he received in the wake of Newport said he was a "sellout, fink, fascist, red—everything in the book." Regardless, *Sing Out!* read the writing on the wall. In their November 1965 issue, they found Dylan's "Baby Blue" encore "fearfully appropriate." The order, they knew, was rapidly changing.

Late in July, Dylan recorded his next single (not released until September), which again reflected his resentment toward those who wouldn't let him go his own way. "Positively 4th Street" was and remains the most vicious song ever to reach the Hit Parade. Whether it was about 4th Street in Dinkytown, in Greenwich Village, or some road of retribution in his mind, it stated Dylan's case plainly. He would not turn back from the course he was on, and with the help of Bloomfield, Kooper, Griffin, bassist Harvey Brooks, and drummer Bobby Gregg, he pounded his message out with a force it had never had before. Harvey Goldstein, Charley McCoy, Frank Owens, and Russ Savakus joined that summer's recording with a new producer, Bob Johnston, and the result, *Highway 61 Revisited,* would still be seen, more than a decade later, as one of the greatest rock records ever made. Dylan's liner notes, now an institution on his albums, were his most haunting and evocative yet. "the songs on this specific record," they stated, "are not so much songs but rather exercises in tonal breath control . . . the subject matter—tho meaningless as it is—has something to do with beautiful strangers. . ."

Forest Hills Tennis Stadium was the scene of Dylan's next public confrontation, at a concert held just days before the release of *Highway 61.* "I have no idea what I'll be doing," he told the *Times* in a pre-show interview. "I'll have some electricity and a new song or a couple or three or four new songs. Time goes by very fast up there onstage. I think of what not to do rather than what to do." The sellout crowd had heard about Newport. A local paper called them "the purists, the socially conscious, the thousands of young boys who grew their hair long and wore rag-tag clothes—as a tribute to their spokesman."

The first half of the show went smoothly, with Jerry White, a folk DJ,

Overleaf:

At Newport in 1965, Dylan's reception was mixed. The battle of acoustic/electric began. Dylan never looked back.
(© Diana Davies/Nancy Palmer Photo Agency, Inc.)

Onstage with Robbie Robertson, San Francisco, 1965. (© 1977 Jim Marshall)

(left to right: Robbie Robertson, playwright and poet Michael McClure, Dylan and Allen Ginsberg, San Francisco, 1965. (© 1977 Jim Marshall)

introducing Dylan, who'd been at the stadium most of the afternoon, watching the overcast skies and 14,000 empty seats. At 9 P.M., in a high snap-collared striped shirt, high-heel black boots, his hair blowing in the wind, Dylan took the stage alone for forty-five minutes. He played seven songs, including "Desolation Row," and left to thundering applause. Backstage, in the midst of cables, packing boxes, and the other paraphernalia of a rock band, Dylan held a conference with his musicians, Robbie Robertson, lead guitarist for a Canadian group called the Hawks, Levon Helm, from the same band, Kooper and Brooks. Anything could happen with the crowd, he warned them. He wanted them to make good music. That was his prime concern. They moved quickly toward the stage.

"There's a new, swinging movement in the country," DJ Murry the K told the crowd, "and Bobby Baby is definitely what's happening, baby!" The crowd's response was guarded, and the band began to play quickly, opening with "Tombstone Blues," then running through an electric "I Don't Believe

You," "From a Buick 6," "Just Like Tom Thumb's Blues," "Maggie's Farm," "It Ain't Me Babe," "Ballad of a Thin Man," and ending with "Like a Rolling Stone." The audience booed, but stopped each time the music started; hecklers yelled, "We want Dylan," "Traitor!" or "Where's Ringo?" whenever there was a clear break in the musical flow. Fans ran for the stage, which was quite a distance from the stands. Dylan never stopped, never acknowledged the chaos of the crowd. His only words, when the heckling got loud, were a somewhat sad, "Aw, come on now."

Concert over, Dylan put down his guitar and left the stadium quickly in the station wagon, Neuwirth driving, Dylan ducking down until they were away from the crowd. Was it his sound? Was it all right? His questions were aimed at the car's occupants and later at the guests at Grossman's post-concert party in Woodstock. In a way he was deriving a lot of strength from stirring up such controversy.

By September, when he played at Carnegie Hall, the tide had turned. Bob Dylan was a rock star, leading (if unwillingly) an American musical movement that would sweep the world. *Life* magazine called the new hitmakers "the children of Bobby Dylan." Protest had gone Top 40 with P. F. Sloan's "Eve of Destruction" sung by exfolkie Barry McGuire, advertised with pictures of him emerging from a fallout shelter. Donovan emerged. Gordon Lightfoot covered "Tom Thumb's Blues." As 1966 melted into the summers of love, the Lovin' Spoonful, lead by ex-folkie John Sebastian, would emerge. In one two-week period at the end of 1965, eighty singles penned by Dylan were released. His monthly songwriting royalty income was being estimated in five figures. Whenever he was asked about the movement he was supposedly leading, Dylan would deny its existence apart from the commercial world he preferred to avoid. "You gotta understand me," he begged, "all my actions are motivated by my conscience."

In September, "Positively 4th Street" was released, rising to Top 10 status by early winter. As Dylan toured, he'd find some real happiness, playing with a group of musicians from Canada, who'd been discovered by both Mary Martin, then an employee of Grossman's, and John Hammond, Jr., son of Dylan's first producer and an aspiring blues player himself. (John, Jr., had played with the Hawks—they'd once backed Ronnie Hawkins—in New Jersey, recorded an album with them and Michael Bloomfield for Vanguard Records in 1964, and worked around New York City after that.) They toured with Bob all that fall.

Part of the process of touring and pop record promotion was an unceasing stream of interviews, press conferences, personal appearances, concerts, and general madness. Everywhere he went, Dylan was being asked to justify himself, give some solid reasons why he'd "abandoned" folk for the supposedly small rewards of rock. Had any of the questioners been given a chance at making successful appearances before audiences of 15,000, and making the kind of artistic statements (and money, honey) Dylan was making, they might have stepped into his shoes without a glance back, but, like prosecuting attorneys looking for controversy, they picked on Dylan's obvious, if unimportant, flaw—his tendency to get booed.

"I'm not the voice of their generation," he told columnist Frances Taylor. "How can I be? I'm not in their generation." Of his old songs, he said, "They're ghosts. . . . I'm writing now for the people who share my feelings. The point is not understanding what I write but feeling it."

Other isolated quotes from interviews during this period add to the impression of Dylan's refusal to bend to the whims of anyone but himself:

"Those old songs weren't simple at all. . . . All these labor people, rich suburban cats telling their kids not to buy Bob Dylan records. . . . 'Which side are you on?' That's such a waste. I mean, which side can you *be* on?"

Or:

"I can't see the future. I hate to think about it. It's a drag to think about it."

Phil Ochs was worried. "I don't know if Dylan can get on stage a year from now. . . . I mean that the phenomenon of Dylan will be so much that it will be dangerous. . . . He's gotten so inside so many people's heads—Dylan has become part of so many people's psyches, and there are so many screwed up people in America, and death is such a part of the American scene now. . ."

William Burroughs, whom Dylan complimented in one interview, met him that fall. "Dylan said he had a knack for writing lyrics and expected to make a lot of money," Burroughs told *National Screw* a decade later. "He had a likable, direct approach in conversation, at the same time cool, reserved. Yes, certainly rather reserved. He was very young, quite handsome in a sharp-featured way. He had on a black turtleneck sweater."

You might call these times his black period. *Highway 61* had come as a revelation to a lot of people, especially those with assumptions about popular music. The aberration known as Bob Dylan had to be taken seriously. Though he'd write great songs long afterward, and though some earlier songs had paved the way, the material he gave the world in 1965 and 1966 had the most importance on a cultural scale, and stands up to inspection a decade later far better than such relative relics as the Beatle's *Sergeant Pepper's Lonely Hearts Club Band.*

If *Highway 61 Revisited* had one obvious lesson, this was it: protest would not change the world. Change yourself and you change the world. It was the romantic notion that provided the fuel for many of the cultural changes of the late Sixties, as masses of people tried to live Dylan's advice. They too had discovered it was "all bullshit" and, like Dylan, they'd try to discover something that wasn't. Baez had called Dylan "a young neurotic." By the standards of society, he was the poet of a generation floundering in neuroses.

After *Highway 61*'s September release, Dylan was as hot as hot got. The record opens with the thundering title single, the song that broke radio's three-minute-length requirement by being six minutes long and too important to cut. "Tombstone Blues" follows, a raging rock song about a dream world populated with characters from Paul Revere, Belle Starr the stripper, and Ma Rainey the blues singer to John the Baptist, Galileo, Delilah, and Beethoven. Single lines, out of context, made clear sense. National banks did sell road maps for the soul then. They still do. But there is no easing the pain of that knowledge. All there is is the tombstone blues.

"It Takes a Lot to Laugh, It Takes a Train to Cry" follows, a tender love song with tinkling piano backup and mournful harmonica solo. Whether the woman he writes of is the same as the "junkyard angel" of "From a Buick 6" we can't know, but the latter is certainly related to the woman of "Love Minus Zero/No Limit." The dream girl returns in "Buick 6" but now she's Dylan's, and she gives him everything and more. Once again, Dylan's imagery is obscure, but meaningful on an emotional level.

He could dissolve himself invisibly in human situations to capture whole ranges of experience. The opening chords of "Ballad of a Thin Man" set the ominous tone of that song about paranoia. The wonder is the ease with which Dylan communicates such an essentially non-verbal situation. "Thin Man" is the clearest evocation of the theme Dylan also treats, differently, in both "Rolling Stone" and "Just Like Tom Thumb's Blues." Is the sword swallower of the sixth verse gay? Is Dylan trying to tell us something about homosexuality, drugs, life? Of course. Are the references intentional? It doesn't really matter, because Dylan conveys more in the tortured "whoooaaa" at the end of "Thin Man" than any veiled reference to heroin or sodomy could impart.

"Queen Jane Approximately," in the same way, was judged by critics of the time to be about Joan Baez and, in many ways, the "advice" Dylan offers in the song fits the situation Baez found herself in after leaving Dylan in London. But at the same time it explodes into the universal situation of a person telling another she's caught in a trap, and he's leaving until she gets herself out. Again, as throughout the album, the force of the words is equaled, and at times surpassed, by the sheer quality of the playing. If the stories he told were sad, the music was celebratory and majestic, and that made the awful words easier to take.

The title track was Chuck Berry-on-LSD, filled with the paraphernalia of modern life, the hype and promotion and gambles of the good old day to day. "You do it, kid, we'll sell it." "You need it, we'll find it." Where? Out on Highway 61, of course. Highway 61 might also have been the street where you could pick up the paraphernalia necessary to "Tom Thumb's Blues," certainly Dylan's most drug-laced song until then, a languorous account of a journey that one interpretation claims is Dylan's early 1964 drive around America. At Eastertime Dylan was in New York, obviously blowing the theory, but one can still see here the results of a pot-smoking drive through America, ending with Dylan's foils failing him, and Bobby Neuwirth and, perhaps, drugs, replacing them as Dylan's protection from the outside world.

Regardless, the song is about pain, as the live version released as the B side of his July 1966 "I Want You" single makes even clearer. Looking back, a few years later, Dylan would say that though all these songs seem to be about others, they were actually about himself, and "Tom Thumb's Blues" is both explanation and rationalization of what Dylan was going through as fame began creeping in on him. Still, each verse is a story in itself, apart from any general theme, and the portrait Dylan paints fills in more of the colors of his world.

"Desolation Row" was the clearest evocation of that world yet. Dylan was talking of life on the barest level. "We come to see the chaos with clarity," Michael Gray wrote, "come to see in the parade a barrage of folk-heroes in careful disarray: participants, victims and agents of a disordered, sick society," turned topsy-turvy by its own inherent contradictions. "Lady and I" begins the tale, and as they walk through this horrorshow world, one is reminded of Nelson Algren's *Walk on the Wild Side,* and the junkie nightmare prose of William Burroughs. Something is wrong on Desolation Row. The lights are going out. The street gets dark in preparation for a carnival, and soon the parade begins, led, quite early, by Albert Einstein, "immaculately frightful," bumming smokes and sniffing drainpipes. Dr. Filth leads a pennywhistle parade. Cassanova is being killed, his power taken away by praise. At midnight, the agents of the factory round up everyone who knows too much and tie them to heart attack machines. Insurance men bring kerosene.

A San Francisco press conference smile. (© *1977 Jim Marshall)*

Nobody escapes unscathed.

Two other songs are part of the *Highway 61* song sequence, though they were not on the album. They were recorded with members of the Hawks—Robbie Robertson, Richard Manuel, Garth Hudson, Rick Danko, Mickey Jones, and Bobby Gregg. (On tour, the drummer was Sandy Konikoff.) Playing with the Hawks was a different experience for Bob. Most of the material recorded with them, prior to the release of *Planet Waves,* was only available to bootleg collectors. "Can *You* Please Crawl Out Your Window," recorded twice, once with the Hawks (soon to be known as The Band), and again for release as a single in January 1966, was one of these. It was the perfect follow-up to "Positively 4th Street," this time more pointed. Phil Ochs told Dylan it was a bad record and lost his friendship for years.

The second song, "Sitting on a Barbed Wire Fence," is, Dylan taunts in the last verse, merely a riff. Four-versed, citing Arabian doctors' shots and a strange woman who fills him with drive, the song concludes that the only way to understand it is to have been in a tunnel and fallen over a barbed-wired fence. In the universe of Dylan's '65 songs, it made a peculiar kind of sense.

It was a Greenwich Village world, ruled by Dylan and his musicians, Bobby Neuwirth, Eric Anderson, Phil Ochs, David (Blue) Cohen, Ramblin' Jack, Dave Van Ronk, Al Kooper, and others. The King had lost his Queen but gained a court that he kept drunk, with Neuwirth paying the bills and making sure the doors of the bars were locked so, if the word got out, the tourists could find Dylan but not bother him. He needed to survive whole, at least with no major chunks pulled from him, and the crowds of admiring folkies saw to that. They followed. They protected. They kept Dylan from feeling the weight of a responsibility that grew greater the harder he looked for freedom.

Dylan was on a burn course. People fed on him. He couldn't stop writing. He couldn't stop the magic. He was too good to be merely a rock star, but lots of people wanted him to be that, even as he tore their hypocrisies apart on his records and, in person, as he'd rip into his coterie of admirers with scathing verbal warplay. Fueled by alcohol, the scenes got vicious. Neuwirth would play jester, Kissinger and Secretary of the Treasury all at once.

The hostility was seen as Dylan's cloak against the loss of privacy and freedom rockstardom demanded. He was not a simple person who'd be made happy with just women, wine and drugs; he hated the crowds he'd inevitably be at the center of. His friends were his competitors, and he was the King, the man with all the bucks and all the bucks could bring. They wanted what he'd gotten by accident, and so his sniping became a protective pose. Others could run with him, but no one could stand in his shoes.

As his songs veered terribly close to frightening, original truths, Jesus was a role for which others seriously contemplated Dylan. No one could share the loneliness he must have felt. He couldn't even get drunk and vomit without someone analyzing the puke for meaning. He was wrapped up in Self: Go inside and you'll learn the truth, and with truth there's no need for religion or philosophy. Such torturous excursions were being met with scorn, and Dylan's defenses were tissue.thin. He didn't like what was happening around him, so he attacked. Kooper, recalling a week in early September when Dylan played electric at the Hollywood Bowl, wrote that Dylan's suite at the Hollywood Sunset was the hub of activity, whether Dylan was eating, talking, reading, or sleeping. One day, trying to get someone off the phone, he pushed an egg salad sandwich into the mouthpiece, followed by an entire

Ramparts **featured Dylan in mid-1966.** *(© 1966 RAMPARTS Magazine, Inc. Reprinted by permission.)*

glass of milk. The room cracked up. Rock stars always provide wonderful entertainment. It's no wonder resentment boiled just under the surface.

In November, Dylan began a national tour, but first he married Sara Lowndes by a State Supreme Court justice in a secret ceremony in Nassau County, just outside of New York City. His marriage to the beautiful model stayed a secret until the story broke the following February. Entirely in character, he denied the event. A few days after the wedding he took off in a private jet for his first official tour with Robertson, Helm, Danko, and company.

More than ever it seemed like everyone was after him. All the magazines from *New Yorker* to *Playboy* to *Esquire* wanted their media pieces as fall turned to winter and Bob's tour took him to the Midwest, where he played the University of Minnesota and visited Hibbing. By December, he was on the West Coast, giving concerts and press conferences, interspersed with the first of a half-dozen recording sessions that would result in 1966's masterful *Blonde on Blonde*. When Fariña saw Dylan in Berkeley, he commented that the singer didn't burn the candle at both ends, rather he used "a blowtorch on the middle."

And always there were the dangling conversations, the inevitable interviews. Between September and December '65 these press conferences and interviews showed Dylan to be an intensely private man, avoiding all attempts at being pinned down (as always), and in doing so, making his forays into the land of journalism pieces of a grander work of conceptual art.

What follows is a composite of moments from all those different Q and A sessions. One was a head-to-head with Paul Robbins from the *L. A. Free Press*, one was a small conference in a bungalow at the Beverley Hills Hotel, one was broadcast in San Francisco, one was a full-scale conference in Hollywood.

Why had he come to California?
"I came to find some donkeys for a film I'm making."
Would he play himself in that film?
"No, I'm gonna play my mother, and we're calling it 'Mother Revisited.' "
Why did he look so tired?
"It's a nervous condition. I look the same anyway."
How many protest singers are there?
"A hundred thirty-six."
Was he sure?
"Well, it's either a hundred thirty-six or a hundred and forty-two. I forget which."
Could he name several protest singers?
"Eydie Gorme and Robert Goulet."
What was his real name and why did he change it?
"I had to change my name from Kanisovich because everywhere I went relatives kept coming around wanting free tickets to concerts. . . . Kanisovich was my *first* name."
Had he really written his first song for Brigitte Bardot?
"That's true."
Why?
"Because I like her."
Why did he like her?

"Why?!?"

Did he mean the songs he wrote?

"Of course not."

What about his teenage fans?

"I don't know what you mean; I have no picture of a teenager in my mind. Name me a teenager. I have no recollection of ever bein' a teenager."

How did he feel about power grabbers and people who'd try to control what you do?

"They can't hurt me. Sure, they can crush you and kill you. They can lay you out at 42nd and Broadway and put the hoses on you and flush you in the sewers and put you on the subway and carry you out to Coney Island and bury you on the ferris wheel. . . . But I refuse to sit here and worry about dying."

Why was rock coming in and folk going out?

"Folk music destroyed itself. Nobody destroyed it. Folk music is still here, it's always going to be here, if you want to dig it. It's not that it's going in or out. It's all the soft, mellow shit, man, that's just being replaced by something people know is there now. Hey, you must've heard rock and roll long before the Beatles, you must have discarded rock and roll around 1960. I did that in 1957. I couldn't make it as a rock and roll singer then."

Had the transition in his life over the previous five years affected him?

"Well, the transition never came from working at it. . . . I'm not going to fake it and say I went out to see the world. Hey, when I left there, man, I knew one thing: I had to get out of there and not come back. Just from my senses I knew there was something more than Walt Disney movies. . . . Okay, so I get the money, right? First of all I had to move out of New York. Because everybody was coming down to see me—people which I really didn't dig. People coming in from wierd-ass places."

Could he still recognize real friends?

"Oh, sure, man, I can tell somebody I dig right away. I don't have to go through anything with anybody. I'm just lucky that way."

If you started with Album One, Side One, Band One, could you watch Bob Dylan grow?

"No, you could watch Bob Dylan laughing to himself. Or you could see Bob Dylan going through changes. That's really the most."

By writing songs instead of poems, was he increasing the chance of reaching his audience?

With French chanteuse Françoise Hardy, Paris 1966. *(© Monique Valentin/ Photoreporters Inc.)*

" . . . All I can do is be me—whoever that is—for those people that I do play to, and not come on with them, tell them I'm something I'm not. I'm not going to tell them I'm the great cause fighter or the great lover or the great boy genius or whatever. Because I'm not, man. Why mislead them? That's all just Madison Avenue selling me, but it's not really selling me, 'cause I was hip to it before I got there."

Did he think of himself as a poet or a singer?

"Oh, I think of myself more as a song and dance man."

Would he stick to folk rock?

"I don't play folk rock."

What did he call it, then?

"I like to think of it more in terms of vision music—it's mathematical music."

Were the words more important than the music?

"The words are just as important as the music. There would be no music

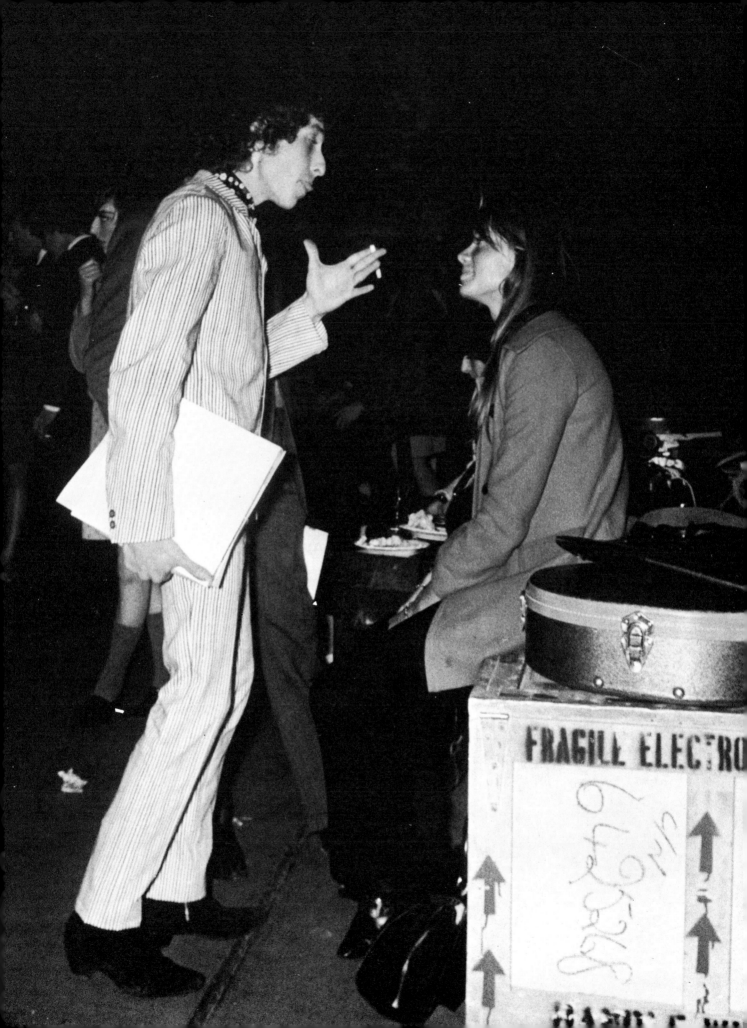

without the words.''

What poets did he like?

"Rimbaud, I guess; W. C. Fields; the trapeze family in the circus; Charlie Rich, he's a good poet.''

If he sold out, who would he sell out to?

"Ladies' garments.''

Could he label himself or describe his role?

"Well, I'd sort of label myself as 'well under thirty.' And my role is to just, y'know, to just stay here as long as I can.''

How would he define folk music?

"As a constitutional replay of mass production.''

Would he call his songs folk songs?

"No.''

Are protest songs folk songs?

"I guess, if they're a constitutional replay of mass production.''

Who is Mr. Jones?

"Mr. Jones, I'm not going to tell you his first name. I'd get sued.''

What does he do for a living?

"He's a pinboy. He also wears suspenders.''

How did he explain his attraction?

"Attraction to what?''

His mass popularity?

"No, no, I really have no idea. That's the truth, I always tell the truth. That is the truth.''

Where is Desolation Row?

"Someplace in Mexico. It's noted for its Coke factory.''

Was he embarrassed to admit his popularity?

"Well, I'm not embarrassed, I mean, you know—well, what do you want exactly? For me to say . . . you want me to jump up and say 'Hallelujah!' and crash the cameras or do something weird? Tell me, tell me. I'll go along with you! If I can't go along with you, I'll find somebody to go along with you.''

A French journal proclaimed Dylan a "New God."

By early 1966, Dylan had sold over ten million records worldwide and had had his songs performed by more than 150 other musicians, including Lawrence Welk. Now he would admit to being a millionaire. Several songbooks had been published; one paperback book was on the stands; a full-fledged biography was forthcoming from Robert Shelton of the New York *Times* (*still* in the works at present); Pennebaker's film from England, now titled *Don't Look Back,* was ready for screenings; *Blonde on Blonde* was being recorded; "Can *You* Please Crawl Out Your Window'' was on the charts six weeks and been withdrawn from circulation; and in April, a new song, "Rainy Day Women No. 12 & 35'' was released for a ten-week stay on the charts that would eventually see it hit #2 in *Billboard.*

"Blowin' in the Wind'' had been released in fifty-eight different versions; Albert Grossman, once a respectable-looking businessman, had taken to wearing granny glasses and a Ben Franklin haircut; and the *Times* and its competing morning newspaper in New York, the *Herald Tribune,* had both published long articles on Dylan's validity as a poet. The more people called him a genius, the cleverer Dylan's remarks became when refusing to comment. No, no, he told one reporter, even Einstein wasn't a genius, no sir, he was a foreign mathematician who would have stolen cars. Dylan in later songs would use that metaphor of the genius as thief.

Bob Johnston, his new, southern producer, had convinced him to record in Columbia's Nashville studios (an idea which, earlier in his career, had been vetoed by the head of CBS—Country), with solid session musicians like Wayne Moss, Charlie McCoy, Ken Buttrey, Joe South, and others. "One of Us Must Know" was recorded with portions of the Hawks/Band. The album was in the works for a long time and they did a few songs at a time. Bob wrote them out in the studio while the musicians played cards. They'd do a good take, then go back to their games until another song was ready. Sometimes, after a few tunes, Bob would go back on the road to tour. It was the kind of life that turns rock stars into burnt-out shells, and it was not leaving Bob Dylan unaffected.

By April, touring was getting him crazy. He apparently resented the heavy schedule he now had as a full-time pop star, and may have resented the people who set it up for him. When Phil Ochs had an encounter with him in Hollywood, he came away saying Dylan was "clinically insane." His general paranoia was increasing, and in what now seems like a horrible warning, both Paul Clayton and Peter La Farge, old Village colleagues, committed suicide, and Richard Fariña was killed in a motorcycle accident two days after the publication of his brilliant first novel, *Been Down So Long It Looks Like Up to Me.*

Life was a constant stream of one-night stands, crowds, demands, and drugs. By the time he left America for the beginning of an international tour, the strain was really showing. And in May he arrived in Paris to preposterous magazine headlines welcoming him as "A Young God." Nevertheless, his music was the best he ever made.

Scandinavia followed Australia. Ireland followed Scandinavia. Then there was England and France and England again. In Australia he took a vicious beating from the press. In England every show was spotted with walkouts. Rick Danko would remember him tuning his guitar for twenty minutes at a show in Liverpool. "Sometimes it's hard to tune a guitar," Robbie Robertson added with a smile. Audiences whistled during the long breaks between songs in Paris. Not quite the conquering hero was he, but still controversial.

Then, at Royal Albert Hall, he gave what many have called the single greatest rock and roll concert of all time. Available on several bootleg albums, the concert soars beyond description. Dylan was living each song as he sang it. Just as on the recording of "Tom Thumb's Blues" from Liverpool that was released as a single, each word of the concert comes off the bootlegs as if etched in acid-pain. The way he sings the word "shot" in "Tom Thumb's Blues" told more about his gut reaction to drugs than any magazine quote.

"Judas," the crowd at Albert Hall screamed at him.

"I don't believe you," Dylan drawled back in his peculiarly hip Midwest wisp of a voice. "You're a liar." One hopes he knew how clear and beautiful the music he was making was. One knows the schizophrenic stardom it caused was hard to bear.

Late in May, he returned to America, polished off the recording of *Blonde on Blonde,* and laid back to await its June release while planning August concerts where previously only the Beatles had dared to tread—the Yale Bowl in New Haven, Connecticut, and the 60,000-seat Shea Stadium. Dylan's contract with Columbia had expired, and the quiet months contained some plotting about where to go, with MGM Records in the lead, offering a million-dollar film-publishing-music deal. Though MGM had been put off by the stories of Dylan's European adventure, he'd become the most

April 29, 1966 saw a tired Dylan hold a press conference on his arrival in Stockholm, Sweden. *(UPI)*

sought-after status symbol the American music business could offer. He had revolutionized the pop business, made literacy an achievement stars could attain, and for the first time raised the pop song to the status of art.

Rock-punk-on-the-edge became, after Dylan, a role many would try to fill, few with distinction. Bob had, simply, become the premier American voice in the most popular mode of artistic communication in history. Now, with his first book about to be released, his ABC-TV show (which Pennebaker had shot with a $100,000 advance for a one-hour Stage 67 special) generating more than its share of interest in a world where TV rock was characterized by "Shindig" and "Where the Action Is," "Rainy Day Women" topping the charts, and the whole country singing about getting stoned, Bob should have been sitting on top of the world.

Blonde on Blonde, thanks to the stimulus of the great musicians Dylan was surrounded with, was an album of letter-perfect rock and roll. Clichés were being invented. Here was an album with a song that lasted *a whole side.* The symbolism was Dylan's, but the situations were everyone's. Gay blades knew just what Bobby was talking about, prototype druggies found justifications in each word. The women always treated Bobby kindly. The songs were bare-boned constructions of real lives, surrounded by chaos. If any one disc recorded in the Sixties can stand as a psycho-historical recreation of the times, this is it. Bob Dylan, at the center of the maelstrom, sent out words that would capsulize experiences so broad as to give that slippery demon "counterculture" its first hints of life. *Everyone* had to get stoned.

Dylan's command of language reached a peak on this, his seventh album. The accuracy of his eye, the smooth slide of his poetry, the ability of his phrases to hit emotion by confusing intellect, all combined to turn songs like "Visions of Johanna" into complete worlds, filled with disturbingly familiar people cast adrift in the trick-playing night. The influence of the Beat poets like Allen Ginsberg, Gregory Corso and others is clear, but the songs defy categorization. "Only when it is amplified by music and declamation," poet Gerard Malanga wrote, "does Bob Dylan's verse stand forth in all its living strength and beauty, in the subtle distinction of its peculiar rhythm. . . . an entirely new language prevails. . . . The happy phrase, daring compression, virile strength, versatility of meter, an astounding wealth of pregnant and purposeful terms, simplicity of construction, an almost unprecedented capacity for the expression of overwhelming emotion and of mysticism, an extraordinary insight into the hearts of the people and their turns of speech—all these characteristics might be enumerated and still the most striking and admirable be left unmentioned. . . . The most notable achievement of Bob Dylan's genius and in which the young poet stands alone, is that for *every* work he coins, as it were, a new language, endows each fresh emotion with a new semblance and a harmony peculiarly his own."

Blonde on Blonde, with its passionate love songs and descents into Dylan's dramatic, urban landscape, is not an album to pin down. Like a "ghost of electricity" howling in the bones of a woman's face, it is more something to feel, something to understand barely as it relates to the man, Dylan, but to understand totally in the sense that one understands that perceived first by the heart, then by the brain. If, as Dylan would write ten years later on *Desire,* "Sad-Eyed Lady of the Lowlands," the obscure, sensuous closing piece of the album, was written in an overnight session at the Chelsea Hotel for muse Sara, fine, but its implications ranged much farther, both for Dylan's

Overleaf:

Onstage at the Olympia Theatre in Paris, 1966.
(© *Monique Valentin/ Photoreporters Inc.)*

(© *Monique Valentin/ Photoreporters Inc.)*

listeners and for the bard himself. This was music made on The Edge. Just The Edge. No, The Edge of *what?* Dylan was peering into what came beyond for hundreds of thousands of people who'd more than likely follow if he said jump. What he found was not pretty. It was real. All too real. As he walked the line, Dylan might have discovered how lonely it was. Once you left the highway, the signs weren't easy to read.

Blonde on Blonde put Bob up against it, and everyone else with him. So sad, so crazy. People wanted Dylan to be their friend and if that didn't work, they bought his albums and "sat around like lamps waiting to be turned on." Where's that at? Desolation Row with the heart attack machines. And that machine was just about to snatch another victim.

Through June, final preparations for *Tarantula* were being made. "It was set for the fall season of 1966," Bob Markel recalled. Five excerpts were to appear in the *Atlantic Monthly,* a prestigious literary digest. A request was made for Dylan to appear and hype the book at the American Bookseller's Association convention as a special feature. Shopping bags and buttons featuring Dylan's face and the word *Tarantula* were made instead, and distributed at the ABA. Described by Dylan in a convention press release as "a series of thoughts as they came to me. You know, not judgments, but comments," he'd worked on it all through the world tour, and people were beginning to speak of the book's debut as publishing's "Event of the Year."

"We'd been conditioned by the publication of John Lennon's first book around the same time," Markel continued, "and we wanted to duplicate that experience of a huge pop star having a little book, published intelligently, become a huge bestseller.

"On, I guess, July 30, I received a call from Albert Grossman's office. They told me Bob had had an accident and was in the hospital, and thus could not attend our planned meeting for the final reading of the galleys. The book had to be delayed."

The afternoon papers carried the story. On July 29, 1966, while riding his Triumph 55 motorcycle, twenty-five-year-old Bob Dylan, "a rock singer living in semi-seclusion near Woodstock, New York," had crashed. He was in Middletown Hospital with several broken neck vertebrae, a concussion, and lacerations of the face and scalp.

5: Stage Fright

"I DEFINE NOTHING," Bob Dylan told *Look* magazine in March 1966. "Not beauty, not patriotism. I take each thing as it is, without prior rules about what it should be."

As he recuperated from the accident, an entire generation set out to live his words. Brother David told them Dylan had cracked his bike up playing on the grass; rumor mongers had it that Bob, tanked up on every pharmaceutical known to man (and now available to every young American with the inclination and the bucks) had gone out on the backwoods roads of Woodstock seeking infinity and damned near found it. He was dead, a vegetable, encased in plastic, or just avoiding the draft, alive because Sara (or Johnny Cash) worried (or followed him to a repair shop), had followed him (or found him). He would never play again. Because he'd been disfigured. Because he was on intravenous morphine, hooked to the Big Fix by folks who knew he knew too much about the agents and the superhuman crew. Hey, hey, LBJ, how many popstars did you kill today?

Whether the new kicks were Monkees or Mothers, something strange always seemed to be happening in the eighteen months Bob Dylan was gone. Something strange like LSD, bananas, Haight-Ashbury, St. Marks Place, Jefferson Airplane, and Moby Grape. Dollar bills burned, and Peace was a dream a lot of people had. There was a first time for everything, be it hearing words like "guru" or reading Marshall McLuhan. You could be out and still Be-In. You could board a magic bus and move further on down the road. You could take leaves, roll them up in paper and see a wild new world. All you needed was love, innocence and mirth. All you got was the power of flowers.

From the Avalon Ballroom to the Boston Tea Party, rock and roll was happening, bursting at the seams, big business obscenely scoring big bucks for a new breed of leather-clad capitalists hiding out as "house hippies" in big corporations, record companies. There were many lies and not a little truth. Janis Joplin and Jimi Hendrix. The Peanut Butter Conspiracy, Sopwith Camel and Brian Wilson's "Good Vibrations." ("There could be mind

gangsters, couldn't there?'' Brian Wilson asked, early in 1967. Somebody should have told him yes.) General Hershey running the draft was the bogeyman. If you walked to the corner you could buy some boogie, and when the boogie ran out there was always nutmeg and belladonna. Soon there was STP too, and the word bummer was invented to cover a thousand possibilities, the loss of a thousand potentialities.

California filled with freaks from everywhere else whose heads were not together, looking for bigger thrills and higher highs. The first Monkees album sold over three million copies in 1967. On Sunset Strip teenagers fought police for the right to dance after 10 P.M. At the University of Wisconsin in Madison, students were asking strange questions about the CIA. At Harvard, a student group called SDS was fighting the war at home.

"Dylan has been doing nothing, absolutely nothing," Robbie Robertson told a reporter. "He's been looking at the gate around his house and training his dogs how to bite." The Hawks had moved to Woodstock and he was also, quietly, playing with them, writing songs, continuing to edit the ABC-TV film of his last tour, which would be delivered seven months late and summarily rejected. *Don't Look Back* premiered in May 1967, in San Francisco, then in September in New York. (Dylan would later try to have the film withdrawn from circulation as a misrepresentation of his character. "Bob hated that movie," his mother would say. "It wasn't Bob Dylan.")

Dylan came close to the edge. In the hospital for a critical week, then in bed for another month, suffering the after-effects of amnesia, mild paralysis, and internal injuries, his recovery was slowed considerably by the lousy shape he was in. The extent of the psychic damage caused by the accident can't be easily determined. In April, to fill the gap, Columbia released a Greatest Hits album. The MGM deal fell through. The TV show was off. *Tarantula* had missed its fall release date.

"Albert's office let me know that the facts and the rumors were very different," Bob Markel said, discussing the period. "He was quite all right, but the trauma of the accident, they told me, appeared to have given him the opportunity for forced rest and reconsideration of his life and work. He was not moving forward in any direction and that was his privilege. I kept that to myself and the months went by."

In the nine months Bob spent in total seclusion, he'd grown to legend status in the newly organized youth culture that seemed to be ruling the world. *Blonde on Blonde* became a gold album, as did *Highway 61, Bringing It All Back Home,* and the Greatest Hits package. Fifty more cover versions of Dylan tunes appeared. People started to squawk about the responsibility Dylan had to his audience, although in *Crawdaddy,* the newly emerged prototype rock magazine, editor Paul Williams wrote, "Dylan owes us nothing. We already owe him more than we can give." The Band moved to a nearby town, to be near their recuperating boss.

In January 1967, a *New York Post* reporter, fueled by conflicting reports about *Tarantula,* headed to Dylan's retreat, "knee-deep in snowdrifts along the tree-covered ridge of Upper Byrdcliffe," in Woodstock, and found a black limousine parked in an open garage. The motorcycle was gone, given to Grossman's gardener. A formidable home, decked out for the Christmas season, with four chimneys, a large barbeque pit, and a gazebo, impressed the reporter as "a vast mahogany stained ski-lodge" offering a "breathtaking panorama of life above it all."

Don't Look Back **appeared in 1967, a vivid portrayal of Bob Dylan, Popstar.**
(Leacock-Pennebaker)

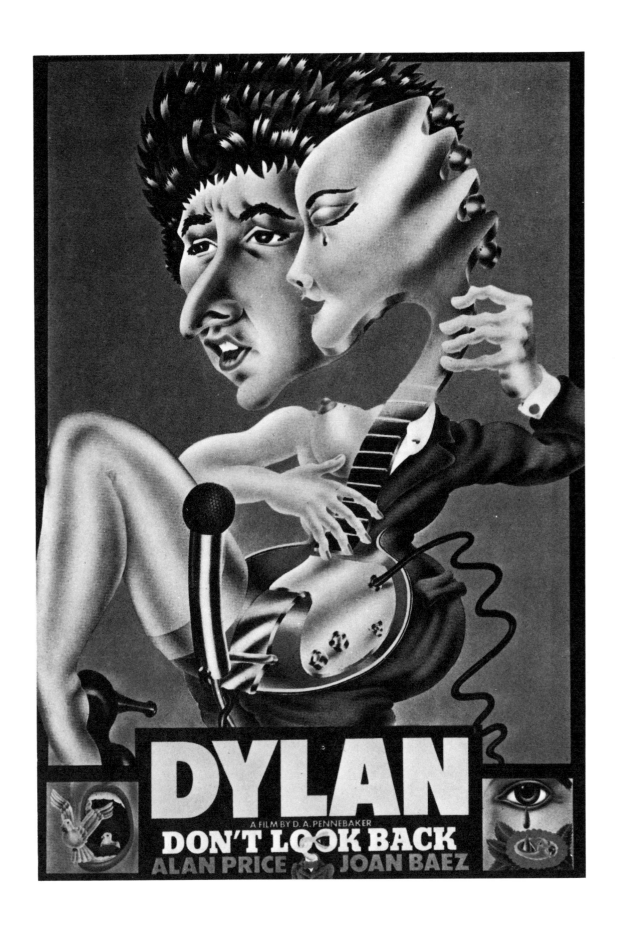

As he stared into the opening door, the writer was confronted with two images. One was of a sedate country house filled with rugs and art. The other was Sara Dylan, in granny glasses, high button shoes and black leotard stockings, shawl over braided hair, screaming at him about trespassing.

The writer, confronted by two large watchdogs, headed for his car, tripped over a tricycle, and drove off, only to be stopped by the local constable. "The Dylans say that you stole the dog's collar," the tobacco-spitting cop said, letting the writer go after a quick search.

Sometime in mid-1967, Al Aronowitz visited Dylan in Woodstock and reported on it in *Cheetah*. He found a charismatic, bearded man in Ben Franklin rimless glasses, sitting under Japanese woodchimes at an electric piano, in his "rambling American chateau of mahogany-stained shingles that clung to a mountaintop above the point where the mountaintop kept its head in the clouds." Dylan, singing new songs, seemed settled.

In May, Michael Iachetta of the *Daily News* decided to seek Dylan out, just prior to the singer's twenty-sixth birthday. After being put off by Grossman's office and by a CBS executive, Iachetta drove to Woodstock where he found the house, the Cadillac in the garage. No, Dylan doesn't live here. The next day he went back; Dylan let him in. He looked "thin, emaciated."

Bob was in one of his expansive secretive moods. Well yes, he'd been keeping up on current events, reading and trying to put his life in perspective; mainly he'd been making more music and writing songs, which was always what his life was about.

And the accident? Dylan finally described how his back wheel locked up and how he woke up in Middletown Hospital all busted up. He'd just recently started moving his neck a month ago. No, he didn't think he'd be driving a motorcycle anymore. A beard and mustache covering part of his face and a blue bandanna on his head hid scars. But Iachetta detected other scars.

And his creativity? Well, the songs were still in his head but weren't getting written down until he'd taken care of some other business, not until some old scores were evened up. And yes, whatever's happening was just fine with him in the music biz, though it was time for another record. (That was a message to Columbia.) The film was done but the book wasn't right yet. Columbia had suspended his contract because he hadn't cut an album yet, but Dylan remained unruffled. Anyway, he just wanted to make music, and as spring turned to summer he did just that, wrapped in a near-inviolable cloak of mystery and rumor.

The Bob Dylan who joined Rick Danko, Garth Hudson, Richard Manuel, and Robbie Robertson (Levon Helm hadn't rejoined them yet) was a vastly different man from the one who'd toured America with The Hawks in 1965. Older, sadder, wiser, he was no longer a screeching post-adolescent, and the songs these men recorded from June to October, 1967, the famed Basement Tapes, show some of the things that concerned this new Dylan.

The changes were organic and natural. They grew from the base of a man who'd run too fast into a brick wall, and lived to sing the tale. "Too Much of Nothing," "Nothing Was Delivered," "You Ain't Goin' Nowhere"—all these songs dealt with Dylan's coming to terms with himself, the life he'd chosen, the life that had been imposed on him, and his incredible talent for combining words and notes. He was being driven into coming up with songs, but they were more or less fun to do.

"I Shall Be Released," "Tears of Rage," and "This Wheel's on Fire" were the first of the tracks recorded that summer to appear, on *Music from Big*

BOB DYLAN

GIVES AN EXCLUSIVE 16-PAGE INTERVIEW IN SING OUT! (OCT/NOV '68 ISSUE)

SING OUT! MAGAZINE, 80 E. 11th STREET, N. Y., N. Y.

SING OUT!
THE FOLK SONG MAGAZINE
VOLUME 18/NUMBER 4—OCTOBER/NOVEMBER, 1968—$1.00

EXCLUSIVE INTERVIEW WITH BOB DYL
INTERVIEW WITH BUKKA WH
TEN YEARS WITH THE RAMBLE
WORDS & MUSIC TO "MR. BOJANGLE
"THE WEIGHT" AND OTHE

Pink, the debut album from The Band. The first set a vaguely apocalyptic tone, as it described a prison whose inmates cried they were not at fault. The last seemed an apt description of the furious months before Dylan's accident. "Tears of Rage" captured the sense of fault that had entered Dylan's universe for the first time. Whereas "The Chimes of Freedom" had spoken of "misplaced unharmful gentle souls" in jail, the prisoners of "Released" did not seem guiltless, and "Tears of Rage," written from a new perspective (a set of universal parents and children), is Dylan's discovery of another way of looking at things. He rages against the difficulty of change. He rages against the force of others' expectations and the brevity of life, how easy it was to waste.

The Basement Tapes, ultimately released in the summer of 1975, tell far more than is superficially obvious about Dylan's state of mind, and his rapidly changing sense of his relation to his art. In the midst of erotic, bawdy, neo-nonsense songs, single lines jump out to define the parameters of Dylan's developing sense of things. The messiah becomes Quinn, the mighty Eskimo (whom the world would love in Manfred Mann's version of the tune), Dylan

At The Newport Folk Festival of 1968, *Sing Out!* unveiled their exclusive Dylan interview in an issue with a cover painting by the singer himself. *(Sing Out! Magazine, 270 Lafayette Street, New York, New York 10012. Used by permission)*

simply a minstrel boy needing salvation, a long time coming, long time yet to come, afraid of going down in the flood, knowing that if he does there is no one else to blame.

The sense of fighting the lure of the void that pervades this group of songs is its most amazing feature. One song cries that "nothing was delivered," promises were made and were not kept, and ultimately "nothing is best." Yet there's still the nonsensical "Million Dollar Bash" to attend, a Mrs. Henry to drunkenly seduce, lessons to learn in order to keep on going, an entire tradition of American folk music, both obscure and obvious, to delve into. In "Odds and Ends" Dylan sings that lost time can't be recovered. How should it be better spent? Perhaps seeking the "Sign on the Cross," perhaps in simpler pleasures like getting your rocks off.

"When there's too much of nothing," Dylan sang, "no one has control." But there was nothing to seek and nowhere to go. Redemption didn't come that easily, guilt was not so simple to deal with, the past couldn't be that easily swept aside. Though the songs were, in part, released, with versions recorded by many artists, something made Dylan unwilling to release them himself. It may have been the basement quality of the recording, done with a small tape recorder and three microphones at The Band's West Saugerties house. As with *Tarantula,* their release would eventually be encouraged by the appearance of bootlegs, but at the time, the tapes were probably used for demonstration only. Dylan's creative process continued, and within weeks, the songs for a new album, *John Wesley Harding,* were ready, and being recorded in Nashville. In October, he taped most of it with McCoy, Ken Buttrey and Pete Drake, following up the two-day session with two additional trips that completed the album.

Which of the rumors were true?

A reporter had come back from Woodstock bearing word from Dylan: "All of them." *John Wesley Harding,* released in January 1968, carried Dylan's real answer, the "key" that the short prose piece on the cover had three kings seeking. The release of the Nashville-recorded, simple, gray-covered album was a strange revelation for that winter when psychedelia had gone suburban; the Beatles had reformed the Word with *Sergeant Pepper;* the Rolling Stones had parodied the Word in the ultimate acid album, *Their Satanic Majesties Request;* several Beatles singles had been added to the soundtrack of their failed television show, *Magical Mystery Tour,* and released as a Christmas album; Donovan had recorded a two-album boxed set of songs for children; the Beach Boys had released *Wild Honey* to resounding critical silence; Jimi Hendrix was setting guitars on fire; Jefferson Airplane were happily and druggily *Bathing at Baxters;* Al Kooper had left the Blues Project to form a new band, Blood, Sweat and Tears; the Firesign Theatre had released their first album; the Byrds had gone country; and people were talking about the Maharishi Mahesh Yogi and a senator from Minnesota named Gene McCarthy was running for President and talking about morality.

Dylan's release of a neo-country disc, filled with economically stated parables and two "redneck country" tunes, was greeted by the public with a fair amount of confusion and a great deal of "What is Bob Dylan trying to tell us?" Coming only a few months after the release of the manic *Don't Look Back, John Wesley Harding* sent listeners into long staring bouts with the LP's scratchy Polaroid cover, searching for the faces of Beatles in the tree branches, the *why* that had to be in Dylan's eyes. To Richard Goldstein, reviewing *Don't Look Back,* Dylan was "Shakespeare and Judy Garland to

Bob appeared in a Johnny Cash documentary in 1969. *(ABC-TV)*

The Woodstock Fair took place in White Lake, but Bob Dylan's shadow hovered over the affair.

my generation," and the bard had come back from over the rainbow to tell us "nothing is revealed."

"Intentional and accessible" was critic Paul Williams' judgment of the album, and the intention began with the real title character, John Wesley Hardin, who, Williams wrote, "at fifteen killed a nigger for being uppity, and kept up that kind of bullshit until 1878," when, at the age of twenty-five, he got thrown in jail for sixteen years. Dylan just took his name, added a "g" (which every critic noted as an apology for droppin' so many gs along the way), and let the world know that a lot of things had changed.

If Hardin was put in jail at the age of twenty-five, Dylan was released. His world was no longer one of chaos without reason. He could have compassion toward well-motivated people who nonetheless did wrong ("As I Went Out One Morning," about the ECLC dinner and Dylan's Tom Paine award). He could express his transition in a dream of St. Augustine, calling on theological imagery as he'd done since his earliest writing, describing himself waking in terror from a dream in which he was among Augustine's killers. He was no longer the self-righteous critic of his earliest days, nor the above-it-all voyeur of the apocalypse of the previous four albums.

When he began, Dylan wrote about morality in a political structure. After 1964, whether because he'd said what had to be said or because he'd gained the commercial freedom to follow his own path, his songs purported to be about love and morality alone, but told just as much, or more, about the political world he was desperately trying to avoid, as they did about himself. He'd learned to spot evil, and as he identified one wrong after another, his descent into unconnectedness went deeper, becoming more and more unreal. His revelation was the meaninglessness of most of the structures of the contemporary world, built as they were on greed, lust, and other evils, and his growing disillusionment with all the wonderful promises America made to its children: promises based on a false political sense of security, promises that eventually had to be broken. Dylan had spent five years and seven albums destroying the claims of authority by telling the truth as he saw it. His ascent to stardom was the good headkeeping seal of approval of those truths. *Blonde on Blonde* was the crowning achievement, Dylan's expression of joy at having reached his adolescent goal. The man who woke up in Middletown Hospital was an adult, looking for "a tree with roots" to strap himself to.

That adult may have been concerned with contracts and debts owed, but his biggest task was the simple act of finding an identity that could comfortably fit into the world. The sense of loss and wasted time that permeates the *Basement Tapes* is resolved on *John Wesley Harding*. Dylan had stripped down to nothing, and now he was building again, this time with the tools of the grown man: compassion and tempered wisdom and the goals of maturity—redemption and then salvation.

Part of the building process was an understanding of what had gone before. In "It's All Right, Ma," Dylan had written of the "lies that life is black and white." By *John Wesley Harding* he'd realized that the past he'd rejected in his black and white days could not be so easily lost. His fierce Judeo-Christian moralism, his equally fierce romantic side, had to be dealt with head on. His role as a single bit of humanity had to be defined. Dylan had to define himself, and *Harding* is the record of the process of discovery.

By declaring his independence from the passing parade, he was, of course, pointing a way for those who would invariably follow, but from now on he would be free of the shackles of expectations and audiences, tied instead to a

YOU'VE GONE TO THE FINEST SCHOOLS ALRIGHT, MISS LONELY
BUT YOU KNOW YOU ONLY USED TO GET JUICED IN IT
AND NOBODY'S EVER TAUGHT YOU HOW TO LIVE OUT ON
THE STREET
AND NOW YOU'RE GONNA HAVE TO GET USED TO IT

personal determinism that would force him to come to terms with his role and
his maligned past before he could again move forward, in critical terms.
Though he was still redefining himself through his art, he'd come full circle for
the first time, and he would (employing a three-dimensional construct of
artistic progress) have to move on the horizontal for a while before again
attempting to climb the vertical. On that horizontal, he'd incorporate his role
as an *American* artist first, then apparently wait for his audience to grow up
and catch up, before returning to his earlier themes and early life of
ambiguous reality, rootlessness, and freedom. For the time being, his sense of
freedom and that of his old audience grew separate. Old expectations would
soon make this "new" Dylan seem imprisoned by himself.

**A radical handbill distributed at
The Woodstock Music and Art
Fair in the summer of 1969.**
(Michael Gross Collection)

At the time of its release, *John Wesley Harding* did not seem like a look back for Dylan. Critic Jon Landau, writing in *Crawdaddy*, found Dylan "prepared more than ever before to accept uncertainty . . . prepared to look at the pieces of reality and let the Miller tell his tale." To Paul Williams, writing in the same magazine, the album was so entirely understandable on an objective level ("Good old rock, expanding our minds . . . Bob Dylan, frontier scout") that the subjective implications became all-important. "All Along the Watchtower," by insisting on questioning the nature of Time, "allows you to think of your life as more than a point on a line." More often than not, critics dealt with the album through discussions of its reliance on country blues instrumentation, fearing, perhaps, that any extensions of Dylan's precisely made points would be too risky. They still thought they were dealing with the same artist as before (though Landau posited the existence of a "new Dylan"), not an appreciably different man looking back on and drawing object lessons from his unique experience of growing up in a fishbowl.

"The day Woody died," Harold Leventhal said, "[Dylan] called up and said, 'Whatever you plan I'd like to be there,' and he was . . ." When it was announced that Bob Dylan would appear at the January 20, 1968, Carnegie Hall benefit for Woody Guthrie, who'd died the previous October, joining Judy Collins, Pete Seeger (whose "break" with Dylan after Newport 1965 was now seen as prophetic of Dylan's "fall"), Arlo Guthrie, Tom Paxton, Richie Havens, Ramblin' Jack, and Odetta, the tickets became the hottest item in New York. Revisionists immediately explained that Bob had never truly left folk music, and had, in fact, been instrumental in its incredible commercial acceptance. And of course, Bob was now a family man, secure with his son Jesse and two daughters Maria (from Sara's first marriage) and Anna, born in 1967.

Lillian Roxon described Dylan's appearance that night as "oddly respectable in his gray suit and open-necked blue shirt." Gentle, mature, and serene were the words used to describe his presence, and his performances of three Guthrie tunes, backed by The Band in rockabilly style, seemed to dissipate former tensions within the folk community.

By February, *John Wesley Harding* was nearing the top of the charts. Dylan's previous singles, "I Want You," "Just Like a Woman," and "Leopard-skin Pillbox Hat" had hit #20, #33 and #81 respectively, and because of that and, perhaps, because his hit singles had been recorded specifically as such, none was released from the new album.

He told a reporter from *Newsweek* he was still into traditional songs, he just used electricity to "wrap it up in"; besides, he was more interested in the song than in its sound. Each song had a moral because of the form in which it was conceived. Slender, smiling, and bearded, he claimed that he subordinated words to music, trying to be a great singer, because great singers, "like Billie Holiday," always made great poetry. He spoke of a new laziness toward songwriting, how the simplicity of the new album helped it hold together, how he was disabled by big cities. He denied having withdrawn; he was a country boy anyway who hadn't recorded because of some contractual difficulties, and who was now aware of his increasing responsibilities toward his family. He used to identify with his songs; now he knew the difference.

Bob Markel also saw Dylan that month, at a meeting held in Albert

The *Self-Portrait* sessions.
(Photo Trends)

Grossman's barn. "The two of us sat and talked for about an hour," Markel recalled. "He drove a car. He looked fine, older, serious. He was far more friendly, far less distracted. He was more grown up and professional, easier to be with. He said he didn't know if he wanted the book published at all. It wasn't something he wanted to improve; it didn't interest him anymore. He'd gone past it. He wasn't sure if he wanted it published as a 'relic' or an unfinished work. I harbored the hope that eventually he'd want this youthful work shown to the public, but left feeling ambiguous about his intentions." Dylan admitted it had no story to others, and only after his accident, when he had the time to read, had he discovered that there were many ways to tell a story.

There were many ways to live a life as well. Nineteen sixty-eight was that kind of year. The battle lines drawn by Dylan, other musicians, and spiritual politicians in the first half of the decade defined those ways. Some people found the answer in murder, and Martin Luther King and Bobby Kennedy fell. Some found it in democratic politics, and Gene McCarthy rose with them, only to fall victim to those who found the answer in toeing the line, be it drawn in Vietnam or Lincoln Park, Chicago. In Paris, the month of May was filled with blood and riot and Danny the Red. In England, in October, anti-war sentiments spilled into the streets of a country that was fighting no war. All the energies of The Summer of Love spilled in a thousand directions after the death of hippie, whether fueled by inertia, drugs or dogma. The Rolling Stones were recording *Beggar's Banquet,* the Doors were at the peak of their popularity, as were Cream, Jimi Hendrix, and the Zig-Zag man. Revolution *was* in the air, even if many of its proponents saw it as a garden party. For a year, it would seem as if the good fight would end in victory. Nixon was the inherent contradiction of capitalism come home to roost. Or so it seemed.

In the spring of 1968, Abraham Zimmerman died and Bob traveled to Hibbing for the funeral. He returned to Woodstock where Sara gave birth to Seth Abraham Isaac Dylan, his second son. In his house, a Bible sat open on a stand. According to his mother, he used it all the time. She said his kids were "climbing all over Bob's shoulders and bouncing to the music. They love music, sleep right through the piano, and Jessie has his own harmonica, follows Bob in the woods with a little pad and pencil, jots things down. This is the way he's chosen to live his life," a simple life, apart from the storm. In June, the release of *Music from Big Pink* again focused attention on Dylan's absence from the scene. For the first time, radical young people began to criticize him for staying away from the fight. The *Saturday Evening Post* ran a cover story on Dylan in semi-seclusion, and the musician renewed his friendship with country singer Johnny Cash. His creativity was being subsumed in a greater need: the need for a good life, the creation of children, the serenity of home.

In June and July, Happy Traum and John Cohen did the first taped interview with Dylan since '66, for an issue of *Sing Out!* that would appear that summer. Bob started talking about *Eat the Document,* the abortive ABC-TV film, and then talked about rock and being on the road in the old days when he had to deliver the goods. Now the audience was different. He expected to keep playing and touring so the time off was not bad for him. Looking back, he said his early career was involved with capturing things in the wind; music was how he made his living. Now he wasn't sure where he was, or where he was going, and he didn't give it much thought.

In the fall of 1969, scraggly bearded Bob made his first network TV appearance on "The Johnny Cash Show."

(ABC-TV)

As far as the *Basement Tapes* were concerned, that stuff wasn't really important. What about all those parables from Kafka? Actually, the only parables he knew were from the Bible.* He said he tried *not* to think about the music business too much; if he wasn't under contract he might quit. He really hadn't wanted to record that last album—he'd been planning to do an album of other people's songs, but he couldn't find enough he liked. Rock and roll was a gruesome ordeal, the touring and all, but he'd done enough to know what that was all about. Now he had time to write and reflect, which was just fine with him. He said he didn't feel any duty to his fans because "the most you can do is satisfy yourself. . . . You can't pretend you're in contact with something when you're not."

He told Happy Traum and John that his contacts with the world were limited now to lumberjacks or artists and not people in academe or critics. Yeah, he knew the movers and shakers of the world, but he didn't really have much contact with them. He was grateful that Grossman had helped him out, that was real stability. As for his views, well at one time people and he saw things the same way, now things are different—he sees what he sees and other people do the same, perspective is all a function of time anyway. It's not groups that change, it's individuals, and that's what Bob was doing.

Late in the year he headed for Nashville again, where he taped a new album, *Nashville Skyline.* It included a duet of "Girl from the North Country" with Johnny Cash that, along with a take of "One Too Many Mornings," was included in the NET documentary film *Johnny Cash, the Man and His Music.* In December he was telling journalists that he was getting control of his energies and finally knew what he wanted with this new album. The songs reflected the inner Dylan, and more basic, closer to home than the stuff on *Harding.* He was hitting his song-writing stride now. However, when the album was released the following May, many critics agreed, but more screamed, "Sellout! Fascist! Fink!" Dylan's appearances in the Cash documentary and on the May 1 premier of Cash's TV show were seen as, at best, tentative attempts to placate rednecks and radicals alike, and at worst, as a total betrayal of principle.

Principle still mattered, though, and to his old fans, Dylan was becoming a problem. Here was this short-haired, suited man on "The Johnny Cash Show" singing "I Threw It All Away," talking about how he'd been mad, never knowing what he had, and only the love that inspired the next song, "Living the Blues," had saved him. *Nashville Skyline* was saying essentially the same thing. It sounded nice, like the best of country music. His voice was different, mellow, not good but nice. "Gotta get back to the country" was the acceptable vibe he sent out. "I'm irrelevant" was the unacceptable one, the one that was telegraphed by his strained manner, the funny grins he shot Cash as they dueted "Girl from the North Country."

"I was scared to death," he said after a recording session the next day. But Nashville liked him, and the rumors of several Johnny Cash/Bob Dylan sessions at Columbia Studios in Nashville had the music world buzzing. In an interview, Joni Mitchell, who also appeared on the show, said, "He used to be better off when he was younger and an angry young man. And he would scream at you and diminish you if he thought your questions were stupid or

*In 1976 he'd name the Bible as both a "best" and a "worst" book in an authors' poll.

unartistic. Now, he knows he can't be an angry young kid anymore. He can't growl. Instead, he stays silent and explodes inside."

By summertime, the "old" Dylan was in the news again, only now because a music festival, taking place in another town nearby, had been dubbed "Woodstock".

Half a million people came to celebrate the Love Generation's last communal orgasm. It wasn't 1967 anymore. Woodstock was an updated Monterey Pop. "That love, peace and granola shit went over real big," David Crosby observed. The Beatles had broken up. The Band, Creedence Clearwater Revival, the Grateful Dead, and a few giant British bands ruled rock and roll. Lost stoned people took lots of illegal drugs, listened to lots of music they'd been sold by Tin Pan Alley even though they bought it at the corner of Haight or St. Marks Place. They tried to forget that in Vietnam poorer and less lucky people than they were dying; in America good people, black and white, were being killed, gassed and harassed by the goon squads; and in Washington, the whole shebang was being run by a crooked slime god, elected by the people of America who, the heads would toke and chuckle, got exactly what they deserved. Egomaniacs preached ego loss, drug dealers peddled the antidote to capitalism at $3 a hit, everyone smiled and grooved on the grand illusion, shooting the bird at anyone who didn't like it, unaware that soon those brave little middle fingers would be bent back, snapped at the knuckle if the body wouldn't fall into line.

In June, SDS had split into several revolutionary factions—White Panthers, Socialist Workers, Friends of Hardhats, and bomb-throwing Weathermen,

Dylan planned to sail to England on August 14, 1969 but one of his children got sick and Bob left the ship with his child in his arms. *(Wide World)*

named after Dylan's first rock and roll single. In July, "Lay Lady Lay" was released as a single and soared into the Top 10, the last of Dylan's hits to reach that goal. On August 2, the Moose Lodge in Hibbing hosted Dylan's ten-year High School Reunion. A delicate-looking Bob, dressed in a loose suit, showed up with Sara, spent an hour, and split when a drunk tried to pick a fight.

That spring Bob had decided against signing a new management deal with Grossman. The "real story" of their parting has never been told, though doubtless it was not a clean break. Bob and Albert would not resume contact until the mid-seventies. Though he claimed he was happy to acquaintances and the press, his three-year hiatus was getting to him. Woodstock had gotten unbearably hip. Grossman was building a cafe/restaurant complex that would cater to the hip clientele attracted to the artist's colony, in part, because of Dylan's presence there. He began looking for a house in New York City, appeared onstage at a Band concert in Edwardsville, Illinois, for one song, and committed himself to appear, at the end of the summer, at a festival in England for a reported £35,000.

The Isle of Wight would be his first paid public performance in four years, and a quarter of a million fans waited until 11:00 P.M. on the last night of the festival for him to appear. Some had flown from as far away as Los Angeles; all waited patiently, lovingly. He was why they were there. They called a campground Desolation Row. Three Beatles and three Rolling Stones came to be near him. Dylan told a London paper he'd come because the Isle of Wight had been Tennyson's home.

At a press conference a few days before the show, Dylan said he was there

By August 27, Dylan was on the Isle of Wight for several days before his first paid appearance since 1966. *(Wide World)*

Left:

Bob and Sara leave London's Heathrow Airport on September 2, 1969. Sara was pregnant. *(Photo Trends)*

Overleaf:

Onstage at the Isle of Wight, Dylan played under an hour and earned a reported £35,000— approximately $67,000. *(©David Redfern/Retna)*

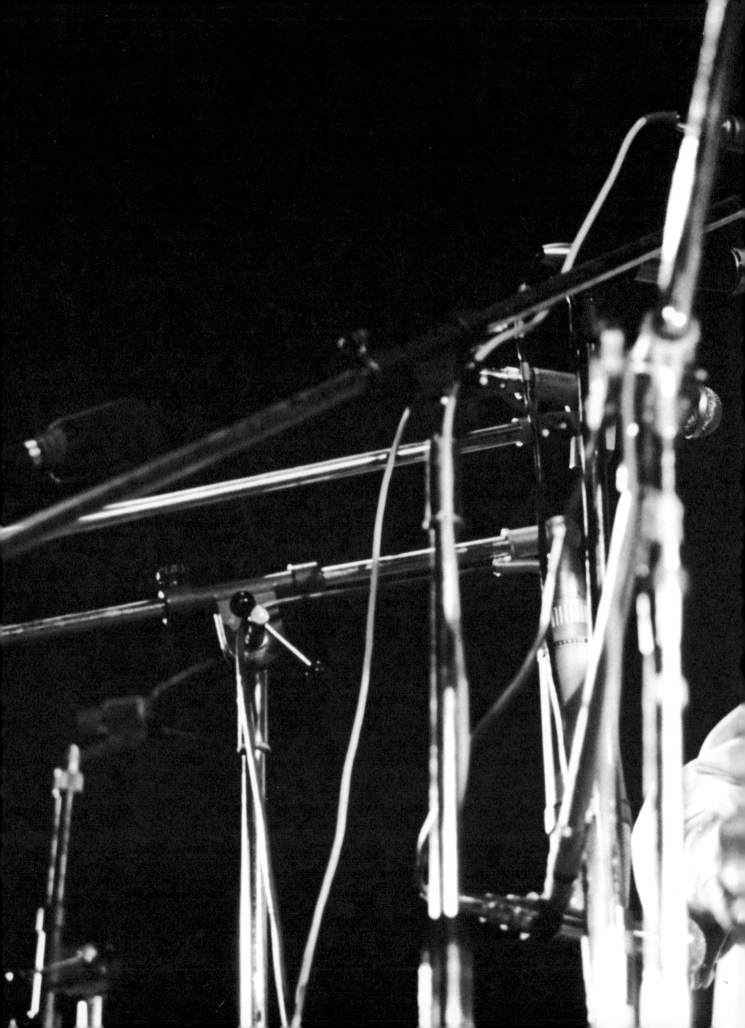

VD WALTZ

Woodstock: 1966

Recording studio 1965

Recording studio: New York 1965

SIDE ONE

* VD BLUES
* VD WALTZ
* VD CITY
* VD WOMAN
‡ MAMA YOU BEEN ON MY MIND
‡ SEVEN CURSES
◊ WILD MOUNTAIN THYME
† EAST VIRGINIA BLUES

* Part of the Minnesota Tape on Dec. 22, 1961.
⊕ Part of the Basement Tape on April 12, 1967 with The BAND.
◊ Part of the Isle of Wight Concert on August 31, 1969.
† Part of the "Scruggs Family And Their Friends" w/E. Scruggs, etc. 1969.
‡ Part of the Witmark Demo Tapes: 1963.

SIDE TWO

⊖ MEDICINE SUNDAY
⊖ TALKING CLOTHESLINE BLU
⊖ I'M NOT THERE
⊖ ODDS AND ENDS
⊖ GET YOUR ROCKS OFF
⊖ APPLE SUCKLING TREE
‡ PATHS OF VICTORY

TRADE MARK OF QUALITY

TMQ 71027

Cover design made for "Trademark of Quality" by "PoPo Productions"

just to play music and if you're going to do your job well, you've got to take care of yourself. At the concert he wore a cream white suit which, with his sparse beard, made him look like a student. One critic described him as looking "tubby." But it was Dylan's night with the Band and he played an hour of mellow, lazy music. Among his seventeen songs were two each from *Another Side, Bringing It All Back Home,* and *Highway 61,* one from *Blonde on Blonde,* "One Too Many Mornings," and eight songs written after 1966. He only spoke five sentences and the performance, from all accounts and several existing tapes, was sloppy, revisionist, yet still gripping.

Sara was pregnant again, and Samuel Dylan was born late that year, after the family had moved into a duplex apartment in a townhouse in Greenwich Village. Dylan was described as searching, troubled, looking for bits of his past and afraid of what he might find. The two older children enrolled in public school, and Dylan fiercely tried to protect the privacy of his family, seemingly aware that it would never be granted to him.

As 1969 wound itself out, leading to the Rolling Stones' wave goodbye to the decade at Altamont Speedway in California, Dylan was in New York, trying to regain touch with his subject matter, integrate his many roles, get back to the streets; the streets, angered, confused, and left wanting by Bob Dylan, had taken it unto themselves to liberate the many tapes floating around and create a new countercultural explosion based, they claimed, on a vision of artistic anarchy and anti-copyrightism—the bootleg record.

In an unrecorded song written at this time, "Wanted Man," Dylan wrote that he might pop up anywhere, even working for someone who didn't know who he was. He'd had all he wanted and a lot more he didn't need. He'd been sidetracked and lost, and now he was simply on the lam. He warned that if anyone saw and recognized him, they shouldn't breathe a word "to nobody." The need for anonymity was as great as the impossibility that Dylan would find it, with albums like *Great White Wonder, Stealin'* and *Talkin' John Birch Society Blues* appearing in record stores with white covers and white labels, making available to the masses such esoteric material as tapes from Minnesota, outtakes from *Bringing It All Back Home,* and live tracks from the Isle of Wight.

Once the dam broke, the flood followed, and seemingly every week, all the way into the late seventies, new bootlegs would come along, mostly by Dylan, then by the Beatles and the Stones and every group capable of selling gold. The bootlegs sold gold too, with *Great White Wonder* selling over 350,000 copies (at prices up to $15 for the 2-LP set) by fall 1970. Though the bootleggers' revolutionary "Free the Music" fervor was lessened by the threat of legal action and some successful prosecutions the next year, they would become an integral part of the music scene, and Dylan's eventual release of the *Basement Tapes* in mid-1975 would still be seen as a reaction to bootleggers.

Dylan's reclusive behavior continued to attract attention in the new decade. Early in the year he began recording a new album. David Bromberg, a guitarist for the tapings, recalled the sessions as "stream of consciousness things," with a lot of improvisation and few songs going past a second take. It was recorded in New York and Nashville.

On May 4, United States National Guardsmen rioted at Kent State University, killing four students protesting Nixon's invasion of Cambodia, effectively ending a decade of student protest in America, turning students toward drugs, communes, and the earliest togetherness groups, based on anything from religion to pop psychology.

Bootleg records first appeared because of the seemingly unlimited demand for Dylan, regardless of quality. Bootleggers claimed to be "liberating" the music. Buyers didn't care.

Twenty days later, Dylan celebrated his twenty-ninth birthday. June marked the release of *Self Portrait,* a slyly titled collection of songs with a front cover portrait from Dylan's own hand and a rear cover photo of the kid pointing his beak up at the sky; it had five new Dylan songs (including "Living the Blues" and "Minstrel Boy"), three old songs recorded live at the Isle of Wight, and over fifteen by others, covering the entire range of traditional American music, stopping to pay tribute to bluesmen, cowboys, hillbillies, and a contemporary folksinger or two. Dylan's mellower voice (which he'd attributed to quitting cigarettes) treated the songs well. The critics savaged him, determined to write him off or bring him back, anything to avoid having to deal with Dylan being Dylan.

In retrospect, the album seems the work of a man with little to say for himself. "All the Tired Horses," the repetitive girl-chorus that opens the album, works around one small joke that provides the thematic direction of the album. Tired horses lie in the sun. Dylan asks how he's to ride them, but "ridin' " when sung sounds like "writin,' " which is exactly what Bob wasn't doing.

"Maybe he's on dugee [heroin]," an *East Village Other* scribe wrote, beginning a rumor that would plague Dylan on and off for years. "This album sucks," the review concluded, echoing the opinions of record buyers who left it sitting in the stores until it was sale priced down to the cost of a single album. "He has brought to *Self Portrait,*" *Rolling Stone*'s second, positive reviewer wrote, "his myth, his images, and his past." *Self Portrait* was his seventh gold album, with orders in excess of $3 million, though, *Crawdaddy* reported, "Bleeker Bob says it's not selling at all in his store."

To continue the confusion, June 9 saw Dylan attending the 223rd Commencement at Princeton University. Eighty-one of the twelve hundred graduating seniors consented to wear formal academic dress. So did Bob, though he left off the tie and mortarboard cap. With him were David Crosby, Sara, and an aide. Dylan hardly spoke to anyone. He seemed nervous behind his sunglasses. He almost left before the ceremony, but stayed, tying a white peace band around his arm before accepting an honorary Doctorate of Music from Princeton's president. His aide said the acceptance was a gesture to the student movement. He left immediately after the ceremony, and spent part of the summer on Fire Island, a resort outside of New York City. Roger McGuinn revealed that he and the Byrds had been asked by Columbia Records president Clive Davis to be on the last album as Dylan's backup. Dylan told him he didn't have too much material, but by the fall he was writing again, both for his own next album and for George Harrison's solo debut.

In the summer of 1970, Harrison got a visa to visit the United States. He came with his friend and ace publicist, Derek Taylor, who wrote of a visit with Dylan their third night in New York. Bob played them his new album, and seemed to Taylor "a decent man, father of five," who looked "as if he doesn't overdo anything."

"He'd gone through his broken neck period and was being very quiet," Harrison told *Crawdaddy*'s Mitchell Glazer, "and he didn't have much confidence, anyhow—that's the feeling I got with him in Woodstock. He hardly said a word for a couple of days." Soon, though, Dylan loosened up; Harrison taught him some chords and Dylan wrote "I'd Have You Anytime" and another song, which he recorded with the ex-Beatle. For himself, he was writing a restless album, *New Morning,* which would mark his critical re-emergence even though it is not remembered as one of his best. Billed by CBS as "A Bob Dylan Masterpiece," and greeted by such respectable rock watchers as Al Aronowitz and Ralph Gleason as no less than a sign from Jehovah that all was right with the world, a gimmickless album of decent tunes, appearing at the height of Led Zeppelin and Rod Stewart rock mania, it marked the end of the period of American domination of the rock scene that had begun, with Dylan, in 1965.

Dylan's "voice was back" the critics said, and he was not using the vocal molasses of his last two albums. An old sense of imagery and word use reappeared, though most of the songs were still celebrations of love, for Sara and the kids. In "One More Weekend" Dylan wrote of traveling alone with his love, leaving the children home. "Time Passes Slowly" was as much a description as a complaint; "Went to See the Gypsy" spoke of a man who could remove fear, "move you from the rear"; and "If Dogs Run Free" asked "Why not me?" If "Winterlude" was a throwback to the earlier material, the title cut seemed to promise that Dylan could and would emerge, somehow, perhaps in the "concrete world" of "Three Angels." And "Father of Night" made it clear that Dylan's mystical sense of religion would not soon depart, the last song on the album, as usual, making a point Dylan wanted people to remember. Bernadine Dohrn, a Weatherwoman in the

underground, even released a communiqué called "New Morning," explaining their new tactics for the Seventies—the successful flight of the Days of Rage terrorists into the underground, where they hoped they could fight without dying.

In October, *New Morning*'s release was greeted with glee by record buyers as well, and the renewed interest in Dylan sparked the release of several underground versions of *Tarantula,* most reproduced directly from stolen, borrowed or lent copies of the galleys that Dylan had been sent just two weeks before his crash. When Jon Landau wrote of "the source of the rock intelligence, the originator of the contemporary rock lyric, the synthesizer, the opera singer, the solo artist, the true outsider; he has so much to live up to, so many expectations to fulfill," a quote came back from Dylan that could be read almost as an agreeing reply. "I don't want to be out front," he said. "I have to keep something in reserve." John Lennon and Yoko Ono were digging primal scream therapy. Dylan was keeping his own counsel, even as tempests swirled around his bearded, sandy head.

In August he'd been reported considering the long-promised Broadway play. In September he was rumored to be rehearsing for a tour. Two months later plans for a television special on CBS were not being denied strenuously.

On June 10 1970, Bob Dylan accepted an honorary degree in music from Princeton University President Dr. Robert F. Goheen, seen here talking to Dylan before the ceremony. Martin Luther King's widow, Coretta King, also received an honorary degree. *(UPI)*

6: Busy Being Born

DYLAN WAS BACK, sort of. At least he seemed to be trying again, writing again, admitting to his restlessness, perhaps doing something about it. He now had five children, a good and beautiful wife, a great deal of money, and a slightly tarnished but still priceless artistic reputation. Something was still wrong, but it wouldn't come into focus, either in his music or his public actions.

In February 1971, *Eat the Document,* the ill-fated *Stage 67* television film Dylan had called "fast on the eye" was shown at the Academy of Music, a dilapidated downtown New York movie theater, as a benefit for a Pike County group fighting strip-mining. Alan J. Weberman, a well-known street person and Dylan fanatic, now calling himself Minister of Defense of his own Dylan Liberation Front, was out front, passing out "Free Bob Dylan" buttons and leaflets that called Bob a junkie.

Jonathon Cott, *Rolling Stone*'s perceptive reviewer, called the film "a private diary, . . . a true night journey through mad, disjointed landscapes." All through it were pictures of movement, constant movement. Dylan says he takes orders from an anonymous telephoner, sings bits of several songs, sits in the back of a car with a stoned John Lennon. It was Dylan seeing himself, and similarities with 1978's Dylan opus *Renaldo and Clara* would be noted.

The *Stone* had other fish to fry though, saying that Weberman couldn't be dismissed as "an overenthusiastic male groupie" because that would be "to completely misunderstand him." They took old A. J. seriously, and at feature length. Dylan had tried to deal with Weberman, and would eventually punch him out on the corner of Bleecker and the Bowery. Weberman's antics caused much information to be released about his idol, but his role was peripheral, like that of a pesky mosquito. Basically Weberman got himself a lot of coverage by picking through Dylan's garbage and writing articles in the underground press about what he found. Then he'd draw up great sociological documents to explain what it all meant. Mostly he succeeded in getting Dylan very paranoid. In January '72, he taped a phone conversation with an angry Dylan who seemed to have much difficulty in dealing with

A bootleg version of Dylan's unpublished *Tarantula,* as peddled on the streets of Greenwich Village early in 1971.

In response to the bootleggers, Macmillan and Dylan finally allowed *Tarantula*'s release in May 1971.

his arch fan/fiend.

That spring, Dylan recorded a single with Leon Russell, Jesse "Ed" Davis, Carl Radle, Don Preston, and Jim Keltner at Blue Rock Studios in New York. "Watching the River Flow," with its rolling rock beat and its image of all-night cafes competing with ever-moving rivers, was another signal of Dylan's return, his re-involvement with the world around him. The wistful longing for excitement was right on the surface, as it was in the contemporaneously recorded "When I Paint My Masterpiece," released by The Band on *Cahoots,* and then, the following November, on Dylan's second hits album (which also included three of the basement tape songs, re-recorded with Happy Traum that October). "Masterpiece," a description of Dylan's travels around Europe with "Botticelli's niece," is also a song of longing for the return of his muse, the coming of his great work.

Late in 1970, Dylan's secretary, Naomi Saltzman, called Bob Markel about *Tarantula.* "As Markel remembers: Dylan asked what I thought of publishing *Tarantula.* He asked me to write a preface. Rapidly thereafter it became a small hardcover book, was sold to a paperback house for over $150,000, and sold quite briskly in hardcover. Everyone who wanted it got it, and as I recall it even made the bestseller lists for a few weeks."

Tarantula was released just a month or so after Toby Thompson's *Positively Main Street* had taken fans back to Hibbing for the first time. By May, when Dylan was to celebrate his thirtieth birthday, stories of a new interest in Judaism (sparked by rumored contributions to the Jewish Defense League, a radical, protective organization run by a New York rabbi) and a trip to Israel ran through the now almost formalized "Dylan Underground."

Bob arrived in Israel in late May. According to the Jerusalem *Post:* "American folksinger Bob Dylan, for a short private holiday with Mrs. Dylan (by El Al)." Reporters who found him out were forced to honor his requests to pass incognito. On his birthday, Israeli CBS ran an ad in the *Post* wishing him a happy birthday, asking him to call. He never did.

He spent his first few days at Jerusalem's Sharon Hotel, but then slipped away, eluding even his travel agent. Found by a reporter on Herzliya Beach, a resort area, he said he'd been "travelin' around all over the place." He said he'd been there before, was writing in his journal, had not written any songs about Israel, but had one about Yugoslavia. Asked about CBS's greeting, he replied he'd seen it, but didn't think they'd really want to hear from him as "my next record won't be released through them in any case." He'd seen a Gregory Peck movie on his birthday, he said, though photographers caught him at one of Jerusalem's most holy places, the Wailing Wall. Asked about a *Time* Magazine article speculating he'd changed his name back to Zimmerman, he said it was "pure journalese and not a word of truth." Finally, about the demonstration that took place in front of his New York home on his birthday, he said, "We can't fence ourselves in—it's a family house with kids coming and going all the time."

(The demonstrators, led by old Weberman, took themselves far more seriously. They carried a cake, decorated with money and hypodermic needles instead of candles, to the front of the house at 94 MacDougal Street in Greenwich Village. No one was home but a little neighbor boy. It was a classic non-event. Dylan's fans were reading in *Time* that *Tarantula* was "less aesthetic achievement than a record of a painful time in an artist's life," and in the *New York Times Book Review* that "an artist who elects to work in a

Stephen Pickering was one of the most productive Dylanologists, publishing a series of pamphlets connecting Bob with the Jewish mystical tradition.

The day before Dylan's 30th birthday, A. J. Weberman, the undisputed king of Dylanology, and a crowd estimated at 400 filled the street in front of Dylan's New York City townhouse for a "pre-birthday party." A. J. (holding microphone) and David Peel (with guitar) were the only entertainment. Bob wasn't home. *(Wide World)*

mass medium communicates in a different way from one who doesn't and must be judged according to his own means, purposes and referants." That review ran with the headline, "The answer, my friends, is still blowin' in the wind.")

"Dylan came to Kibbutz Givat Haim (which means 'hill of life')," writer Eve Brandstein recalled, "with an interest in bringing himself, Sara and the children to the kibbutz. The only thing was he wanted to get a guest house, have the kids go each day to the kibbutz for the experience, but that he and his wife would not have to work on the kibbutz. Rather, they'd stay in a guest house and pay for the stay and the keep of the children. He wanted to put some time in—I think at least a year. He was turned down by a woman named Pdut, head of the volunteers who came each year in return for the kibbutz experience. He wanted special privilege and they were afraid that if word got out of the kibbutz would be overrun. They were terrified of what might occur.

"I was in the hills that day, and we heard he'd been there, seen all the facilities, been knocked out by the guest house situation, and wanted his kids to have the experience. He was spotted all over the place, finally ended up taking a villa in an exquisite part of Israel and staying in Herzliya for several months, maybe longer. He examined the lifestyle, but, and I don't know why, decided not to make the commitment."

"He came several times," recalled Jeff Labes, a musician also in Israel at

MUSIC SCENE

Ladies and Gentlemen, Bob Dylan!'

by Nigel Kime

Photo: courtesy C.B.S. Records

Somewhere, there must still be some people who don't know what all the fuss is about. For all the thousands who flocked to Earls Court and to Blackbushe aerodrome, there are many more thousands to whom DYLAN is just a five-letter word which they may have seen in the national dailies, together with photographs of a scraggy, scrawny 37-year-old singer in dark glasses. For those people, I feel sympathy: I feel that they have missed out on something. For me, 1978 has been the year of an event that is guaranteed a permanent place in heart and memory. After fifteen years of listening to the Man on record and watching him on film and video, the chance arrived to witness him doing what (I am now convinced) he does best—the live concert.

The story begins on Cup Final Saturday 1978: as Ipswich are holding on to their 1-0 lead, I am on a pavement in Leeds preparing for a lengthy wait. In eighteen hours time, tickets are to go on sale for six concerts to be performed by **Bob Dylan** in six weeks time. After twenty hours I am actually holding them in my hand. It is impossible even to try to describe the mixture of excitement and confused disbelief that overtake me at this point. Perhaps only an Ipswich supporter would have even the vaguest idea of how I feel.

Two and a half months later and I find myself in the midst of a quarter of a million people at an airfield in Surrey. In the meantime I have spent two nights at Earls Court Exhibition Hall, being invaded by the greatest musical experience, surely, in the history of the medium. Over ninety thousand people had shared that experience, and here again at the Blackbushe Picnic, there are 250,000 coming back for more. Certainly, something is happening here, and I think I know what it is.

It has been said that Dylan's voice alienates more potential listeners than it wins. Admittedly, at times it is uncomfortably high-pitched and pained, but there is also another dimension of power and emotional intensity which makes it the only possible vehicle for his songs. There

certainly can be no doubt as to his song-writing abilities: compositions such as *Blowing in the Wind, Mr. Tambourine Man, Like a Rolling Stone, Just Like a Woman, All Along the Watchtower* (and many, many more besides) are already a part of our cultural language.

Through such songs Dylan has worked a unique influence over a generation (or, in fact, several generations). Without actively shaping thought or ideas he has encouraged thought and ideas; he has encouraged people to look around and inside themselves, and to strive for understanding and awareness. Do you remember Jimmy Carter's Inaugural Speech? Sometimes even the President of the United States admits a debt to Bob Dylan.

The songs are of paramount importance, and at the 1978 British concerts they are delivered with respect and affection—with alterations musically and even lyrically adding to their contemporary relevance. With the new treatments they sound even better than before.

But what is most striking—either in the darkened vault of Earls Court, or the balloon-festooned monster arena of Blackbushe—is Dylan's peerless stature as a rock performer. His total control over the material—drawing every possible ounce of impact from his voice and lyrics—his total control over his sizeable (there are eleven of them) band of musicians, his every move: it's all so magnetic, it's very nearly hypnotic. Every member of the audience is compelled to watch, compelled to absorb every word this man is saying. *"And every one of those words rang true, and glowed like burning coal. . . . Like it was written in my soul."*

In many minds Dylan is a figure very much associated with the 1960's: in other words, a spent force. In some respects that is true. Possibly he will never again have the same degree of impact that he had back then when he came along with guitar and harmonica and turned the world upside down. But that definitely does not mean that he has nothing left to say. Like Neil Young, who in many minds is synonymous with the Sixties by virtue of his *After the Goldrush* album (and is still delivering the goods with the new *Comes A Time*), Dylan's relevance is established for all time. His reworking of old songs, his recent compositions (if you missed the concerts, *Street Legal* is the next best thing) mean that there is still time to lend an ear to his work. Although a man with a past, unlike Jimi Hendrix—to whom he poignantly dedicated *All Along The Watchtower,* and whose former glory is recaptured on the excellent *The Essential Jimi Hendrix*-Dylan is still capable of going forward.

Performances of two and a half hours at Earls Court and three hours at Blackbushe are enough to convince me that there are enough natural resources in Bob Dylan to keep us fuelled with thought and entertainment for some years to come.

Come and join us.

Photo: Pat Mantle

Viewed from Scotland
by R. J. McCafferty, MOD Glasgow

BY the time members receive this edition of "Red Tape" a few points which I wish to clarify may have been aired at Conference, however, as Dispersal is such an important issue may I take this opportunity of stating the views of my Branch and the overwhelming majority of Civil Servants in the Strathclyde region in regard to this vexating issue?

For some time now, most of us have been aware of the Government's plan to Disperse jobs from the London area to the provinces. By and large the Dispersal of those jobs has been effected with minimum hardship. There do exist, however, some problems in connection with the Dispersal of jobs to certain areas, in particular Cardiff and Glasgow. These have been termed "Disputed areas". The problems affecting Dispersal to Cardiff have to a great degree been "ironed out". But the issue of Dispersal to Glasgow remains highly contentious for one reason or another.

To date I have yet to hear one valid argument against Dispersal of jobs from the London area to Glasgow. After speaking to London based Civil Servants I find that logic and fact make little headway against myth. The stop-at-nothing tactics employed by certain people in the Metropolis only reinforce the growing mood of cynicism felt by Provincial Civil Servants regarding the Civil Service hierarchy. 392

Frankly, some of the "baloney" perpetrated, in opposition to Dispersal, would be laughable if it weren't so serious. Let me give a few examples.

No Redundancy

Because of some misleading comments and circulars etc., emanating from CPSA HQ a considerable number of members still believe there is a redundancy threat for people who do not wish to be dispersed. For the misinformed I advise them to read our Annual Report 77/78 under the sections dealing with Dispersal and Redundancy. Mr. Charles Morris, Minister of State for the Civil Service has given a categorical assurance that there will be no redundancy for non-mobile staff involved in Dispersal. (Reading between the lines you will also note that Ken Thomas our General Secretary is endeavouring to link the no redundancy guarantee of Dispersal to that of the Manpower Economies Exercise. It is apparent that he is prepared to sacrifice the Dispersal Programme to achieve that guarantee. His aims are honourable, his methods are not!)

Unemployment

CPSA propaganda on this subject would lead us to assume that because unemployment levels in London have risen slightly the Hardman Dispersal Programme is no longer feasible. Rubbish!! The Annual natural wastage rate in London is 20,000-plus (that's over

20,000 vacancies created each year). In the MOD, at any given time there are 500–700 Clerical Officer vacancies in the London area, these are jobs which cannot be filled. The situation in London is so desperate that candidates who fail the short answer test are being recruited (another case of double standards). One other example to illustrate Metropolitan chaos is the fact that the MOD have recently issued a vacancy notice requesting Clerical Assistants throughout the UK to transfer to London. Ludicrous, isn't it?

Efficiency

It has been claimed that by Departments being split this will reduce efficiency with a loss of "face to face" contact. In a survey reported by Hardman between 31% and 49% of existing "face to face", contacts could be as efficiently dealt with by "narrow band" communications, i.e. audio systems. He went on to say that such systems are effective, acceptable and economical where reasonable sizes of Dispersal provide contacts of this nature. There would also be greater efficiency due to the reduction in the pressure of commuting between home and central London. In this day of high technology we could put an office (perhaps the CSD?) on the Moon and still remain in constant, efficient communication.

Expense

The costings by Government clearly indicate that the Dispersal Programme will, notwithstanding the capital cost of new buildings, produce considerable long term savings to the National Exchequer, i.e. Land and office premises cost considerably less than in Central London. Civil Servants working in Glasgow will be paid less for doing the same job in that there will be no London Weighting. A better calibre of staff can be recruited in Glasgow, pound for pound, than in London. Projected costs do not include the enormous savings in Social Security and Unemployment benefits made by the influx of Civil Service jobs and the subsequent creation of ancillary employment.

(cont'd p. 394)

time. At one point, he investigated a Yeshiva, "exploring the possibility of entering it, the students there said. It was for *ba-al tshuvah*, repenters, those who returned and became ultra-orthodox Jews. It's a lot of acid-freaks who study Talmud and Torah all day," learning the 613 mitzvos, or rules of traditional Judaism. "He was almost unrecognizable, short-haired and fuzzy. He was checking things out. Anytime a Jew goes to Israel it has to be a mystical experience."

Back in New York, he appeared with George Harrison and a cast of thousands at two Madison Square Garden benefits for war-torn Bangla Desh. His presence was a definite surprise, though a speed freak sat in the aisles of the press section, snorting methedrine from a plastic bag, muttering as he bounced on the concrete steps, "Dylan's coming, Dylan's coming." Most of the audience were more like the two girls who screamed "PLAY LAYLA" at guitarist Eric Clapton through the entire show. Then the speed freak stood, yelling, and Harrison introduced a friend and though the name was obscured by the roar, it couldn't have been anyone else but Dylan. Jesus and Gandhi doing a duet of "Satisfaction" couldn't have gotten an ovation like Dylan did, as most of the audience screamed, seeing the skinny little man in the bluejean jacket singing his guts out for the first time on an American stage in years. The man with the stage fright was doing his greatest hits, backed by the all-star band, and he was doing them justice, doing them like they mattered. The twenty-minute ovation made the Garden shake. The album and film of the event confirmed Dylan's return to an identifiable, comfortable persona. His face, though slightly bearded, was not "tubby." His voice was high and somewhat snarling. The songs sounded real to both author and audience. The clenched fists he raised after his set were comforting, but strange.

In November, *Greatest Hits Volume Two* was released, followed in rapid order by the single "George Jackson" and, in December, by an entire live side from *The Concert for Bangla Desh*. The single, recorded in both electric and acoustic versions, reflected a statement Dylan had made in the mid-Sixties. He'd read Jackson's *Soledad Brothers* and had been moved. Thus the song was seen as a sop to those who called him a sellout, and a further example of his quiet retention of conscience to those willing to follow where he chose to go. He portrayed a world made of nothing but prisoners and guards, and Jackson was behind the bars. *Ramparts*, a well-respected New Left Magazine, said that the song "completes the rehabilitation of Bob Dylan."

In the fall of 1971, poets Peter Orlovsky and Allen Ginsberg were giving a reading to which Dylan sort of drifted in, standing in the back. Later in the evening Dylan and Ginsberg got together and started improvising blues lyrics which cracked them both up. They eventually recorded an album of what Ginsberg would call gaylib rags. Ginsberg went on to say that, in the old days, Bob told him, he used to go into a studio, chat up the musicians, babble into a microphone and then rush into the control room to see what he had. Then he'd write it down, arrange it, and sing it again. To *Melody Maker,* the English music journal, Ginsberg said, "I don't know if he's getting any more into political things, any more than he ever was, 'cos he always was socially concerned." The Dylan/Ginsberg collaborations were sold to Apple Records as *Holy Soul Jellyroll,* and ultimately released in 1974 on a small label.

On his 30th birthday, Dylan went to the west Wailing Wall while visiting Jerusalem with Sara. This photo of him adjusting his yarmulke gave credence to the reports he'd been actively bankrolling the radical Jewish Defense League. *(UPI)*

Bob leaves The Mariposa Folk Festival in Canada under police guard. *(B.I.C. Photography Ltd.—Bruce Cole)*

In July 1972, Bob, hidden beneath hat and shades, appeared at a reception following a Rolling Stones concert in New York. *(New York Post photograph by Vernon Shibla. © 1972 New York Post Corporation.)*

Right:

New Year's Eve 1972 saw Dylan join Robbie Robertson and The Band for four songs at their midnight show at New York's Academy of Music. *(UPI)*

Through 1972 however, Dylan was projecting an extremely low profile, though he appeared as a session player on a number of records released through the following year, including backup piano on two cuts from Steve Goodman (credited to Robert Milkwood Thomas). He also made major contributions (credited as "Bob Dylan") to *Doug Sahm and Band* including a new, previously unrecorded country waltz, "Wall-flower," and he played harmonica on Roger McGuinn's first solo album ("Oh, Mr. D., I'm so restless"). He told one reporter during the time he wasn't playing with anyone; it was the year of Richard Nixon, a good time to be busy doing nothing.

In February, the first Dylan biography appeared, to a review in the Sunday New York *Times* that called Dylan a shadow, "existing not in the world but in the mind, [a creature] of collective need."

Here and on the following pages are a series of photos of Bob as he appeared in Sam Peckinpah's *Pat Garrett and Billy the Kid.* "Alias," as he was called in the film, co-starred with James Coburn and Kris Kristofferson. *(Metro-Goldwyn-Mayer, Inc.)*

By the fall, Dylan was involved in the production of a new Sam Peckinpah film, *Pat Garrett and Billy the Kid,* a tale of an outlaw pursued by a monomaniacal lawman in a time when the West was losing its lawless image, getting somewhat civilized. Dylan was being advised at the time by Kris Kristofferson's manager, who'd helped arrange the Isle of Wight concert. It was suggested that Dylan join Kristofferson and James Coburn in the film, written by Rudy Wurlitzer for the director of *The Wild Bunch* and *Straw Dogs.* Dylan talked to Wurlitzer, screened *Wild Bunch,* and went to the set in Durango, Mexico, to check things out.

He arrived late in November, dining the first night on roast goat at Peckinpah's home, and the next day visited the set, looked around, tried on costumes and hats, and sang a song called "Billy the Kid" to Sam, Kris and Coburn. He was offered the part of Alias, one of Billy's sidekicks, on the spot. Told the part could be expanded, he apparently declined, and though he'd ultimately appear in a good portion of the film, he had only a few lines. He spent the last month of 1972 and the first two months of '73 in a house in Durango with Sarah, the five kids, and a dog named Rover. The kids had a ball while Bob worked.

On the set, Dylan was as mysterious a presence as he'd been for the past several years to the music world. He didn't talk to writers, which the publicist for the movie thought a bit strange. He shared a trailer with Kristofferson but sometimes went for days without uttering a word.

Screenplay writer/author Wurlitzer knew that Dylan came down to learn about the movie business. But on the set Dylan was close to anonymous. Kristofferson, who'd been a janitor at CBS studios in Nashville when Dylan recorded *Blonde on Blonde,* loved working with him and praised his incredible energy. And he loved the way Dylan could play any sort of guitar style from flamenco to bossa-nova to folk. In the film though, Dylan's presence was disquieting right from his first scene, appearing in a printer's apron at his initiation in Billy's gang, where he was asked his name.

"Alias." His body twitched. He tapped a knife against his leg.

"Alias what?" a bad guy demanded.

"Alias whatever you want," outlaw Bob answered, in a smooth motion tossing the knife into the neck of another desperado.

A reporter for *Creem,* then gaining credence as the punky alternative rock magazine, called Dylan, as they panned the film, "a big-nosed, oatmeal-voiced pipsqueak," bragging about his past statement that the only thing a journalist could do with Dylan in 1973 was hit him. *Creem* concluded

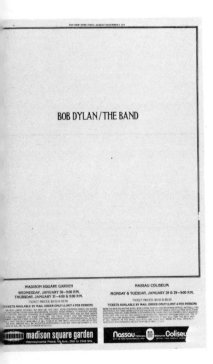

BOB DYLAN/THE BAND

MADISON SQUARE GARDEN
WEDNESDAY, JANUARY 30—9:00 P.M.
THURSDAY, JANUARY 31—4:00 & 9:00 P.M.
TICKET PRICES $9.50 & $8.50

NASSAU COLISEUM
MONDAY & TUESDAY, JANUARY 28 & 29—9:00 P.M.
TICKET PRICES $9.50 & $8.50

madison square garden   Nassau Coliseum

At the close of 1973, the announcement of a Dylan/Band tour appeared in newspapers across America.

in a burst of critical blindsight that Dylan had become a has-been "reduced to playing bit parts on his friends' records, appearing in their movies in minor roles."

There were possible reasons for his behavior. For one, Dylan's contract with Columbia had run out after the release of *Pat Garrett and Billy the Kid,* the movie's soundtrack, and for another there were royalty problems, as Columbia owed Bob a fortune in back royalties and had a great deal of unreleased material in their vaults. Now, in early '73, his options were open; he left Mexico and moved to a rented house in Los Angeles. The members of the Band had all moved to the beaches around Malibu, California, and were also at a breathing point in their careers. To keep busy, Bob produced an album for Barry Goldberg and did the backing vocals. He also backed Booker T. and Priscilla Jones on harp in their Malibu-recorded *Chronicles* album.

Since mid-'72, Bob had been checking out record companies, and by May '73 Clive Davis, then president of Columbia, was refusing to talk about Dylan's situation. According to a record executive at Warner Brothers, Dylan, in a meeting around mid-'72, appeared to be uncertain about what he wanted to do and having trouble centering his creative energies. Now he began an association with David Geffen, a fellow Malibu resident, who owned Asylum Records and recorded special artists like Joni Mitchell, Jackson Browne and the Eagles. In November Dylan entered Village Recorders in Santa Monica with the Band to record *Planet Waves* for release the following January. In apparent retaliation, CBS released *Dylan,* a generally disgusting collection of outtakes from the *Self-Portrait* period, which not only did nothing for his reputation, but also took sales from the Asylum LP; it included a song called "Sarah Jane" that opened with the privacy-dispelling line, "I got a wife and five little children," and was actually one of the hotter tracks on the disc.

On the other hand, *Planet Waves,* a sexy rocking album, indicated the merger of Dylan's old adolescent spirit with self-conscious maturity. He was singing here as Everyman who understood both his common humanity and his relationship to that humanity's definition of reality, a reality *he* saw as far from simple, often ambiguous in the extreme.

"Forever Young" in both fast and slow versions was a beautiful song to his children, his audience, and himself, a prayer for achievable immortality. "On a Night Like This," "Tough Mama," "Hazel," "Something There Is About You," "You Angel You," and 'Never Say Goodbye" were all fiercely erotic songs, gritty enough to be about real women. "Dirge" and "Wedding Song" were terribly candid expressions of Dylan's own emotional life. "Dirge" especially, with its references to his accident, could be about his attempt to pull together the strands of his own life. In "Going, Going, Gone" he wrote of being at "the top of the end," not caring what happened to him next. The acceptance and strength displayed through the entire album resolutely supported the words of Dylan's liner notes which began, "Back to the Starting Point!"

Beginning January 3, 1974, Dylan came back so strong he dominated the thoughts of thousands upon thousands of people. His 1974 tour was like a steamroller. What follows, a portion of an article written that winter by Michael Gross for the Vassar *Miscellany News,* captures as well as any city-by-city description what that tour was like:

Onstage in Boulder, Colorado.
(© Robert Shaw)

Backstage in Boulder, Bob plays ping-pong. *(© Robert Shaw)*

Bob walks to the stage in Fort Worth, Texas. *(© Robert Shaw)*

Then it was 1974 and an ad appeared in the New York *Times* announcing an appearance and tour by Bob Dylan and The Band, all ticket requests to be sent by mail to "BOX LUNCH" at an address in New York City. A rock critic, living in the funky country, I saw the ad and knew to move fast, calling the proper publicity person in the proper Record Company High Rise to beg a seat for my little paper, writing an envelope to "BOX LUNCH" with my free hand. I read reviews of the opening shows in Chicago and prayed. The answer came back from the East Coast Publicity woman.

"Maybe." Drool, fool.

A few weeks later the envelope came from "BOX LUNCH." The seats were closer to a Twinkie and a sip of diet cola, but they were

seats, nonetheless, at Nassau Coliseum on Long Island, the worst concert hall in creation, where they tried to make kids stay seated at Alice Cooper concerts and would bust you for wearing a Jack Daniels T-shirt. A day later, two more tickets came, this time from Gwen, the Knicks' manager's secretary. They were for Madison Square Garden. They were great seats. I made a blind date and let memories of Bob Dylan dance in my head.

The drive to Nassau was slow. Cars passed filled with kids who looked like they'd been hibernating since the last Vietnam Peace Parade; more still passed filled with kids who must have listened to Dylan in their cradles. Kids who'd been too busy looking over their shoulders for the heat to speak out against the madness.

(Bob Gruen/Elektra/Asylum Records)

The seats were in an area cocky critics in their orchestra places usually called "The Gods," a good mile from the stage. Bill Graham, the man who put the tour together, was so far away he looked like a guitar pick with legs. The crows looked like they wished it was a Grateful Dead concert and the rent-a-cops looked like they wished the kids would be gratefully dead.

Dylan appeared, and though the crowd roared, he could hardly be seen or heard. The sound drifted over the seats with all the clarity of a symphony heard from inside a spinning washing machine. The show was a drag from beginning to end. The crowd screamed for "Like a Rolling Stone." They didn't recognize "Ballad of Hollis Brown." The hype was too great; expectations like mine couldn't be met.

In the midst of the show a girl came pushing through the aisles giving away incense.

"Hey man," she said in a drawl half Hicksville, half Hari Krishna. "Listen. Like y'know when Bob told George that he was gonna do these shows y'know like George asked us all to go out and like see if like all the people would like contribute to help feed the uh starving children y'know 'cause like George is into that and Bob still is but doesn't want anyone to know but couldn't you give me a dollar 'cause like y'know Bob wanted George to have us do it and well if you don't have a dollar couldja spare some change?"

She took back her incense and walked away, carrying it and the death of the English language. Her feet were bare. "Like a Rolling Stone" was coming from the stage. I wondered if she knew Hattie Carroll? If I should risk my dreams to see Dylan again? Of course I did and discovered a whole 'nother level. The voice at the Garden was still mannered, affected, strained. He did the old songs with feeling, but a different feeling. Different enough to send you out thinking how you'd write about Selma or Medger or Andrew, Michael and James. The edge was gone; some sadness remained. It wasn't contrived, though. One thing Dylan has always found are things you could hold like a handful of rain and never defy. He was sinister and sentimental, fragile and freezing. The encores that night were "Maggie's Farm" and "Blowin' in the Wind." They seemed new. Standing there singing them was a man with a dissected life, songs torn to shreds. But he'd done it. He made time disappear.

He played forty concerts by mid-February, went to shows in clubs, seemed happy, secure, back into music. At the last three shows in L. A., all but one track of a live album, *Before the Flood,* were recorded ("Knockin' on Heaven's Door" was from New York), and the album, released in June, was a storming document of a tour for which twenty million people had requested tickets for the 651,000 available seats.

To *Rolling Stone,* Bob was expansive and happy. Yes, he saw the daylight and went for it. To *Newsweek* he explained that Saturn had entered his astrological universe a long time back, and had just left. He didn't know it at the time, and if he had he would have gone and hid. Those things just hang out there in your life and screw things up. Now he was clean and free. There'd been some unfinished business, but that was all over now. He'd been reborn.

Onstage at Madison Square Garden in New York. *(Michael Gross)*

7: Riding for Isis

BY AUGUST 1974, Dylan had left Asylum Records. At a record business convention three years later, David Geffen would recall, "He said 'I don't want to sign a contract, will you take my word on it?' I thought, Bob Dylan, the guy who wrote 'Blowin' in the Wind' and 'The Times They Are A-Changin'"—I trusted him. And he fucked me." Later that day Geffen retracted, saying Dylan "didn't come through."

He re-signed with Columbia Records. During the fall, he recorded an album in New York with Eric Weissberg's group, Deliverance. Publicity men at Columbia thought they had a winner and started previewing it for selected critics. However, over Christmas in Minneapolis, Dylan decided to re-record half of the ten songs with a group of local musicians. The new album, entitled *Blood on the Tracks,* was released in January. It was the first record since *Harding* to completely captivate his long-time fans. Some felt it was a return of sorts to 1965 because he was again writing musical vignettes about himself.

Blood on the Tracks was filled with beautiful melodies and catchy tunes which had potential for hits as singles. Lyrically it was astounding as well, opening with "Tangled Up in Blue," which many took to be a parable of Dylan's married life. The story was one of an affair in which the two protagonists skirted each other, playing around with each other for years, drawing closer, then further away, finally parting with the singer vowing to "get to her," having realized their differences and his need. "Simple Twist of Fate" was a slower tune, about an affair with "my twin" that began in a park, continued in a strange, bare hotel room, and culminated with the singer walking the waterfront, knowing and feeling "too much within," blaming his sadness on the twisting of fate.

"You're a Big Girl Now" finds the singer speaking to a woman who's grown and left him behind. Continuing his ever-present fascination with the weather, Dylan sings of being "back in the rain" while the woman is dry. "I can change," he cries, "I swear." But the woman is gone, having found the change in the singer's weather too much to bear. He wants her back, but seems to realize that his changes won't be bent to her will.

"Idiot Wind" was an epic, a searing look at the price paid for fame, intensely personal, universal for just that reason, as Dylan sings of "the pain I rise above," a losing warrior who awakes to find himself a victor, soiled, wary, and a little vengeful. The fight was not just with his audience, his friends, his wife. Rather it was with life, as it had always been with the very best of Dylan's songs. If it ended with a verse about love, all the better, for there, in the misunderstandings between two people, was where Dylan always found his most telling situations.

Side One ended with "You're Gonna Make Me Lonesome When You Go," a perfect song of fleeting love, echoed in the cry of "Meet Me in the Morning," where Dylan begs his "honey" to return to him.

The Jack of Hearts drove into a town where trouble was brewing in "Lily, Rosemary, and the Jack of Hearts," the rambling narrative that followed. Lily, the princess of the dance hall, falls for him, angering Big Jim, the owner of the diamond mine, whose ring she wore. Rosemary, Jim's wife, felt ready to die, wanting to go out big. The Jack was creating a storm, Lily's arms around him, "jealousy and fear" lurking nearby. Down the street, the Jack's gang was cleaning out a bank, and in the cabaret, Big Jim shot the Jack. Rosemary stabbed Jim and was sentenced to die, and Lily was left in the empty cabaret, thinking of her father, Rosemary, the law, and above all, the Jack of Hearts, a murdered thief.

"If You See Her, Say Hello" was another wistful love song, very much in the tradition of "Girl from the North Country," again finding the singer left lonely, wishing it wasn't that way. "Shelter from the Storm" seemed like the story of the woman who left—the story, one had to assume, of the love of Bob and Sara, who met in a different, scary time, came together because she gave him a roof, some relief, some peace, and split, leaving the singer in the position of bargaining for salvation, offering his innocence, and begging for another chance. Given Dylan's artistic history, it's clear that, should she not give him shelter again, he'd be back in the horrible world he'd once known. It's also clear that the differences between them are, even in the singer's mind, so great as to be unresolvable.

"Buckets of Rain," the closing song, is a romp, a proposal, and a bit of advice: "All you can do is do what you must." If, as many said, Sara and Bob had been having problems, then *Blood on the Tracks,* in the depth of its honesty, its searching for understanding, may have kept the marriage together for a while. "Imagine him singing those songs to you," a girl asked on first hearing the album. "Wouldn't *you* go back to him?"

"Up to Me," a song contemporary with the *Blood on the Tracks* tunes, wound up on Roger McGuinn's post–Rolling Thunder tour album, *Cardiff Rose.* The song is about a fourteen-month separation between a man and a woman. She disappeared. He had a wasted affair with a woman named "Estelle." Now he's searching for her, telling her their story in hopes of getting her back, exercising his option of playing on her love, taking responsibility for his actions, which mirrored his sentiments on *Tracks.* The album was released in three different covers; the liner notes by Pete Hamill on the major one made a good point: Dylan was only a troubadour after all, a minstrel in a great tradition of artists, and he was a survivor.

On March 23, 1975, Dylan joined a multitude of musicians at a benefit organized by Bill Graham for cultural activities in San Francisco's high schools. For forty-five minutes, backed both by members of The Band and

Follow You Down," "Hazel," "I Don't Believe You," a reprise of "Baby Let Me Follow You Down," and "I Shall Be Released" with the whole crew joining in. At this writing, *The Last Waltz* was Dylan's last public appearance onstage "I've been with those guys a long time," he said that evening.

On February 19, 1977, *New Musical Express* reported spotting Dylan in Paris with Robert Rauschenberg and Dotson Rader at the opening of the Pompidou Center of Art.

Early in April, the New York *Post* reported that "In a court in Santa Monica, Calif., Sara Shirley Lowndes Dylan . . . was granted temporary custody of the couple's five children, in the first action in her suit for divorce. Mrs. Dylan, who is 38 years old, also was granted exclusive use of their home in Malibu pending trial . . ."

By early May *Rolling Stone* had unearthed her court statement and had spoken with The Band's manager, Larry Samuels, in Malibu.

David Blue, Lanie Kazan, Robert DeNiro and Ronee Blakely join Bob at Blakely's appearance at Los Angeles' Roxy, March 1977, just after the announcement of Sara's intention to divorce him.
(Brad Elterman)

Dylan, Sara's statement said, had moved a "strange woman named 'Malka' " into a guest house on the grounds of their Malibu estate. Sara discovered her "unexpectedly sitting at the breakfast table in the company of our children and Respondent, apparently enjoying herself," causing the children to become "greatly disturbed." She went on to describe Bob's "bizarre lifestyle."

"In the past several weeks Respondent has been continuously quarrelsome. He constantly looks at me menacingly . . . and orders me from the house. . . .he wants me out so that 'Malka' can move in." The court gave Sara the house in the beginning of a divorce action that could see Dylan forced to give her half his assets, under California's community property laws, as well as child support and alimony.

According to Samuels, Bob and Sara are still very much in love, even though Bob has a tendency to get a little over-amped because he's "a wacked-out Gemini" and because he's so volatile, having the capacity to be a different person every day. Samuels maintained it was all old stuff and would resolve itself eventually. And Dylan, spotted with friends in the Roxy in L. A. one night after the action was filed, was said to be cooperative and smiling. Rumors flew that he was being courted for a new record deal by ex-Columbia president Clive Davis, now head of Arista Records.

Early in May, Jerry Weintraub, President of Management III, a multi-faceted entertainment firm specializing in talents like Frank Sinatra and John Denver, announced his company's signing of Bob Dylan for personal representation. Tour plans for late 1977 were said to be among the topics of their first meetings. Dylan was overseeing the editing of the Rolling Thunder Revue film, and planning other movie and television projects.

The Rolling Thunder docu-drama was directed by Dylan and Howard Alk, constructed in Malibu from four hundred hours of footage shot on the road. Tentatively entitled *Renaldo and Clara,* the movie was for a time rumored to be one of the issues in the ongoing divorce drama of Bob (Renaldo) and Sara (Clara).

"It's very much a poet's film," Dylan was quoted in *New Musical Express. Los Angeles* reported that the four-hour film included forty-seven songs. Dylan is played by Ronnie Hawkins and Sara by Ronee Blakely. Joan Baez is "the Woman in White" and Allen Ginsberg is "the Father Figure." Characters from songs cross with those from real life in Renaldo's dream constructions, and one self-styled critic described it as "nonlinear," reflecting Dylan's description of his first personal venture in film, the "quick on the eye" *Eat the Document.* Yet advance notices could be easily doubted, just as the doubters of Hibbing, U Minny, 4th Street, Forest Hills and Isle of Wight seem, through the passage of time, to have become irrelevant. Since 1966 Dylan's desire to work with film had never wavered. The effort of a decade was not easily dismissed with a wave of a "nonlinear."

Dylan had come full circle. In a burst of publicity, *Renaldo and Clara* was released and Dylan was again the subject of press scrutiny, more willingly, in fact, than ever before. His sunglassed mug graced the cover of *Rolling Stone* and he had his second *Playboy* interview. He promised tours, albums and more, his creative output again placing him atop the heap of popular American musicians. For Dylan was again proving he was something else, something special. A Voice. A Consciousness. A man with a continuing vision of his life and ours, not merely a top pop attraction, our greatest living poet, budding filmmaker, or artist of the high wire, but all those things and more.

In the audience at Eric Clapton's winter 1976 appearance at the Los Angeles Forum. *(Brad Elterman)*

Lynn Goldsmith's remarkable series of portraits of Bob Dylan in early 1976 were taken while Bob recorded "Buckets of Rain," with Bette Midler, in New York City. *(Lynn Goldsmith)*

Chronology

1940

Smokey Robinson born

1941

Joan Baez born

Robert Allen Zimmerman born

1942

Cassius Clay born

1943

LSD synthesized

1945

United States population 139,928,000; per capita income $1,223.

Yalta Conference held by British Prime Minister Winston Churchill, U.S. President Franklin D. Roosevelt and U.S.S.R. Premier Joseph Stalin

Death of President Roosevelt. Vice President Harry Truman becomes 33rd President of U.S.

Benito Mussolini killed by Italian partisans

Suicide of Adolf Hitler in Berlin

German army surrender at Rheims. V-E Day proclaimed

Potsdam Conference attended by Prime Minister Churchill and subsequently Prime Minister Clement Attlee, President Truman and Premier Stalin; establishes a four-power authority of the U.S., U.S.S.R., Great Britain and France

U.S. drops atomic bomb on Hiroshima. Japan surrenders. End of World War II

Lend-Lease Act, which cost U.S. more than 48 billion dollars, ends League of Arab States organized

United Nations Charter ratified by 29 nations

War Crimes trials begun in Nuremberg, Germany

Bob Marley born

International Bank for Reconstruction and Development (World Bank) formed

Black Markets dealing in food, clothing and cigarettes, appear throughout Europe

1946

U.S. government takes control of striking railways and coal mines

Philippines gain independence from U.S.

U.S. Supreme Court rules unconstitutional segregation of blacks on interstate buses

Jean-Paul Sartre's *L'existentialism est un humanisme* published

U.S. Atomic Energy Commission created.

Pilotless rocket missile constructed

Chester Carlson invents xerography

1947

President Truman outlines Truman Doctrine of economic and military aid to countries threatened by Communism

Congress passes Taft-Hartley Act; prohibiting use of union funds for political purposes, outlawing closed shop and strengthening government's position in strikes and lock-outs

More than one million U.S. World War II veterans enroll in colleges and universities under G.I. Bill of Rights

Henry Ford dies, leaving substantial portion of fortune to expand philanthropic activities of Ford Foundation

U.S. first to fly airplane at supersonic speed

1948

Charter of Organization of American States (OAS) signed by 21 American republics

U.S. Selective Service Act, calling for continued military draft, passed

Mahatma Gandhi assassinated in India

U.S. Congress passes Marshall Plan, allocating over 5 billion dollars for European recovery

Jewish state of Israel formed

Berlin blockaded by U.S.S.R. Western powers institute airlift

U.N. General Assembly adopts declaration of human rights with prevention and punishment of genocide

Representatives from 147 churches and 44 countries meet in Amsterdam to form World Council of Churches

World Health Organization established in Geneva

Recession increases and unemployment grows in U. S.

Polaroid camera developed by Dr. Edwin Land

Sexual Behavior in the Human Male by Albert C. Kinsey published

1949

North Atlantic Treaty Organization (NATO) formed to safeguard Atlantic community against threat of aggression by U.S.S.R.

Republic of Ireland proclaimed in Dublin. Great Britain recognizes independence

Apartheid program declared in South Africa

Communist People's Republic of China formed at Peking with Mao Tse-tung, Chairman, and Chou En-lai, Foreign Minister

Philip Hench discovers cortisone

U.S.S.R. tests its first atomic bomb

U.S. launches guided missile to 250 miles above earth's surface

The Club, a discussion group-meeting place of Abstract Expressionists founded.

Television production resumed after war. One million household TV sets in use in U.S., up from ten thousand in 1946

1950

U.S.S.R. and People's Republic of China sign 30-year pact in Moscow

Beginning of Korean War

Chiang Kai-shek becomes President of Nationalist China (Taiwan)

Senator Joseph McCarthy advises President Truman that State Department is riddled with Communists and Communist sympathizers

Congress passes McCarran Act calling for severe restrictions against Communists in U.S.

U.S. recognizes newly-established state of Vietnam with capital at Saigon; signs military assistance pact with France, Cambodia, Laos and Vietnam

U. S. reports 480 million of world's 800 million children undernourished

1951

General Douglas MacArthur, relieved of his commands in the Far East, protests Administration's policy in address to Congress

23.5% of all U.S. homes have T.V. sets, up from .92% in 1946. Color TV first produced in U.S. Transcontinental television inaugurated

1952

Dwight D. Eisenhower elected 34th President of the U.S.; Richard M. Nixon, Vice President

Jackson Pollock completes *Blue Poles*

Great Britain announces production of atomic bomb. U.S. begins hydrogen bomb tests in Pacific

Contraceptive pill produced and marketed

U.S. Nautilus, first nuclear powered submarine, launched

1953

Joseph Stalin dies, succeeded as Premier by G. M. Malenkov.

Nikita Khruschev appointed First Secretary of Central Committee of Communist Party of U.S.S.R.

Julius and Ethel Rosenberg tried and executed for espionage against U.S.

Korean armistice signed. U.S. and Korean mutual defense treaty effected

1954

U.S. Supreme Court rules segregation in public schools violates 14th Amendment

Senator Joseph McCarthy attempts to prove Communist infiltration into U.S. Army. Senate formally censures him

U.S. signs pact with Nationalist China

Bob Zimmerman's Bar Mitzvah held.

Billy Graham's evangelical meetings in U.S. and Europe draw capacity

Inoculation of children with anti-poliomyelitis vaccine begun in U.S.

Solar battery developed by Bell Telephone Company converts sun's rays into electricity

With 6% of world's population, U.S. has 60% of cars, 58% of telephones, 45% of radios and 34% of railroads

Public concern grows in Europe and U.S. over fallout and disposal of radioactive wastes

1955

First formal meeting of independent African and Asian states

Blacks boycott segregated Montgomery, Alabama bus lines

Nicholas Ray's *Rebel Without A Cause* released, starring James Dean. Dean dies in crash

First atomically generated power produced, Schenectady, New York

"Rock Around The Clock" reaches #1 on charts

1956

At 20th U.S.S.R. Communist Party Conference, Nikita Kruschchev denounces Joseph Stalin

Gamal Abdel Nasser elected President of Egypt, seizes Suez Canal. Anglo-French forces bomb Egyptian airfields; U.S. and U.S.S.R. pressures effect cease-fire; U.N. fleet clears Canal

U.S.S.R. troops invade Hungary. Martial law and mass arrests follow

Alan Ginsberg's *Howl* published.

U. S. sends aid to Israel

Martin Luther King emerges as major black leader; advocates passive resistance to segregation

Dangers of nuclear radiation subject of World Health Organization Report

Elvis Presley's "Heartbreak Hotel," his first #1, released

Transatlantic telephone service inaugurated

1957

France, West Germany, Italy, Belgium, the Netherlands and Luxembourg sign Rome Treaty beginning Common Market

Joseph McCarthy, U.S. Senator from Wisconsin, dies.

International Atomic Energy Commission established

Eisenhower Doctrine formulated to protect Middle Eastern nations from Communist aggression

U.S.S.R. launches Sputniks I and II, first earth satellites

Jack Kerouac's *On The Road* published

1958

Arkansas Governor Orval Faubus defies Supreme Court school desegregation order by closing public schools in Little Rock and reopening them as private schools

Nikita Khrushchev declares attacks by U.S. on People's Republic of

China will be interpreted as attacks against U.S.S.R.

U.S.S.R. grants loan to United Arab Republic to build Aswan Dam

Buddy Holly appears on Ed Sullivan Show.

Vice President Nixon received with open hostility on goodwill tour of South America

Unemployment in the U.S. exceeds 5 million

Beatnik movement, originating in California, spreads throughout U.S. and Europe. Beginning of widespread use of drugs

1959

Fidel Castro ousts Cuban President Fulgencio Batista and becomes Premier

Charles de Gaulle inaugurated as President of France.

Vatican Council, 20th ecumenical council of Roman Catholic church (first since 1870), convened by Pope John XXIII

Bob Dylan leaves Hibbing

U.N. General Assembly condemns apartheid in South Africa

U.S.S.R. Lunik I reaches moon; Lunik III photographs moon

U.S. Post Office Court declares D.H. Lawrence's *Lady Chatterley's Lover* unobjectionable

Buddy Holly, Richie Valens and The Big Bopper die in plane crash.

1960

U.S. Blacks initiate sit-in campaign at lunch counters in South

U.S. Congress passes Civil Rights Act to safeguard voting and other civil rights of Blacks

John F. Kennedy elected 35th U.S. President; Lyndon B. Johnson, Vice President

Caryl Chessman executed in California

Brasilia, new capital of Brazil, created by Lucio Costa

Francis Gary Powers shot down over U.S.S.R. U.S. admits to aerial reconnaissance

U.S. experimental rocket-powered airplane travels at nearly 2,200 m.p.h.

U.S. scientists develop laser device

Heart pacemaker developed

1961

U.S. severs relations with Cuba. Bay of Pigs invasion by exiled Cubans with U.S. backing, fails

Berlin Wall constructed

Beatles debut at Cavern Club, Liverpool

President Kennedy establishes Peace Corps

Bob Dylan debuts at Gerdes Folk City, New York

Actions of conservative John Birch Society concern U.S. Senate

Yuri Gagarin orbits earth in U.S.S.R. satellite. First U.S. manned space flight by Alan Shepard

Satellite Telestar launched from Cape Canaveral, enables transmission of live T.V. pictures between U.S. and Europe

Conference regarding preservation of African wildlife held, Tanganyika

World Council of Churches advocates birth control due to Worldwide population explosion

1962

U.S.S.R. and Cuba sign trade pact. U.S.S.R. installs missile bases in Cuba

Ban the Bomb demonstrations in England

U.N. finds approximately 44% of world's adult population of 1.6 billion illiterate

Dylan appears at Carnegie Hall Hootenanny

1963

Nuclear testing ban signed by U.S., U.S.S.R., Great Britain, and 93 other countries

President de Gaulle objects to Great Britain's entry into European Common Market. Britain rejected

Dylan appears on BBC-TV, England, at Newport Folk Festival; Carnegie Hall.

200,000 Freedom Marchers gather in Washington, D.C. Violent civil rights demonstrations in Birmingham, Alabama. President Kennedy calls out troops

The Beatles "Please, Please Me" is their first #1 hit.

President Kennedy assassinated. Vice President Johnson becomes 36th President of U.S.

The Feminine Mystique by Betty Freidan published

U.S. Supreme Court rules unconstitutional state and local laws requiring recitation of prayers in public schools

Nobel Committee inquires into moral impact of TV on young

1964

People's Republic of China challenges leadership of U.S.S.R.

President Johnson signs Civil Rights Bill into law

Dylan tours with Joan Baez, plays Philharmonic "Halloween Concert"

U.S. destroyer allegedly attacked off North Vietnam; U.S. bombs North Vietnam

Cassius Clay wins World Heavyweight Championship, becomes Muhammed Ali.

Martin Luther King awarded Nobel Peace Prize

U.S. Surgeon General's report, Smoking and Health, links lung cancer with cigarette smoking

1965

Malcolm X, Black Muslim leader, fatally shot in New York

Simon Rodia dies, creator of *Watts Towers* in Los Angeles.

Legislative momentum for anti-pollution laws gains on national scale in U.S.

Bob Dylan films *Don't look Back*, switches to electric music, releases "Like a Rolling Stone."

President Johnson signs Medical Care for the Aged Bill into law

Beatles awarded MBE's, play Shea Stadium in New York

Race riots in Watts district of Los Angeles

Byrds hit #1 with "Mr. Tambourine Man."

Pope Paul VI visits N. Y. to deliver peace appeal to U.N. General Assembly

Jefferson Airplane form in San Francisco

2.63 million high school graduates out of 3.52 million 17 year olds in U.S.;5,921,000 students enrolled in colleges and universities; 709,200 degrees awarded: 551,000 Bachelors, 140,000 Masters, 18,200 Doctorates

1966

Chinese Red Guard demonstrates against Western influences

Lenny Bruce dies.

Dr. Michael DeBakey, in Houston, Texas, implants plastic arteries leading to an artificial heart

Dylan crashes motorcycle in Woodstock, drops from view, re-signs with CBS

Timothy Leary forms LSD religious cult. LSD banned.

Andy Warhol's *Chelsea Girls* film released. Beatles retire from stage.

Bill Graham opens Fillmore Auditorium

"Ballad Of the Green Berets" tops U.S. pop charts.

Richard Fariña dies in motorcycle crash.

Woody Guthrie dies

1967

King Constantine and family flee Greece after military take-over

Otis Redding dies

Diggers mourn death of "Hippie, loyal son of media," San Francisco

Che Guevara dies

Rolling Stone founded

First Be-In held, Golden Gate Park, San Francisco

Six Day War fought between Israel and Arab nations

Beatles release *Sgt. Pepper's Lonely Hearts Club Band*

Thurgood Marshall sworn in as first Black U.S. Supreme Court Justice

Don't Look Back premiers

Dr. Christian N. Barnard performs first human heart transplant, Cape Town, South Africa

Monterey Pop Festival held

Nationwide demonstrations against Vietnam War: 50 thousand protestors to Washington, D.C.; Martin Luther King leads march in N.Y. Angry Arts against War in Vietnam, a week long demonstration by artists, poets, actors and musicians in N.Y:C.

$17 billion spent for alcoholic beverages in U.S.

Doors release "Light My Fire"

1968

Martin Luther King assassinated in Memphis

Dylan appears at Woody Guthrie Memorial Concert

Robert F. Kennedy assassinated in Los Angeles

Marcel Duchamp dies

Riots and police brutality mark Democratic convention in Chicago

Otis Redding's "(Sittin' On) The Dock Of The Bay" reaches #1

Action Program—freedom of press and expression of minority views—proclaimed in Czechoslovakia by First Secretary Alexander Dubcek. U.S.S.R. and Warsaw Pact troops invade Czechoslovakia, arrest Alexander Dubcek and reestablish direct press censorship. Czech leaders accede in Moscow to U.S.S.R. demands to abolish liberal policies and to have foreign troops stay indefinitely

Stanley Kubrick's *2001: A Space Odyssey* released

Richard M. Nixon, promising to end Vietnam War, elected 37th President of U.S. with narrowest margin since 1912; Spiro Agnew, Vice President

Tarantula bootlegs and excerpts appear

Crimes of violence in U.S. up 57% since 1960

Hair opens in New York City

Student unrest worldwide

Jacqueline Kennedy weds Aristotle Onassis, Greek shipping magnate

Certain food additives linked to cancer in laboratory experiments

U.S. Navy intelligence ship Pueblo charged with violation of North Korean waters, captured. U.S. protests

1969

Fighting erupts in Northern Ireland. British government sends troops.

Fighting erupts in People's Park, Berkeley. California governor Ronald Reagan sends troops

Inflation becomes an international problem

Judy Garland dies

First women generals named in U.S. Armed Forces history

Led Zeppelin appear at Newport Folk Festival

Woodstock Music and Art Fair attracts more than 300 thousand young people. Traffic snarls and drug arrests mark event

Dylan records in Nashville with Johnny Cash, appears with him on TV, plays Isle of Wight.

U.S. Supreme Court Justice Abe Fortas resigns upon disclosure of dealings with convicted financier

Sharon Tate and others murdered by Manson Family

448 American universities closed or on strike due to campus revolts precipitated by Vietnam War

Meredith Hunter dies at Altamont Speedway Rolling Stones concert

Diane Linkletter dies

Brian Jones dies

Jim Morrison arrested for "lewd behavior" following Doors concert in Miami

Charles de Gaulle resigns as President of France

John Lennon and Yoko Ono begin Bed-In For Peace, Montreal

Apollo XI lunar module lands on moon. Astronaut Neil Armstrong first man to stand on moon.

Great White Wonder, first bootleg LP, appears

1970

Arab commandos hijack 3 jet planes bound for N.Y. from Europe. Hijacking becomes international problem until strict security measures enforced at airports

Jimi Hendrix dies

Chicago Eight trial ends

Janis Joplin dies

National Guard kills four Vietnam War protestors at Kent State University

FBI battles Black Panthers

Dylan receives Princeton honorary degree

U.S. stock market declines. Dow Jones Index drops to 631. The price of gold falls below official price of $35 an ounce

Tarantula published

Millions of Americans participate in anti-pollution demonstrations to mark first Earth Day

Women artists picket *Whitney Museum,* demand equal representation

231 million TV sets in use in U.S.

Ringo Starr records in Nashville

1971

Dylan appears at New Year's Eve show of *The Band*

26th Amendment to U.S. Constitution lowers voting age to 18

Eat The Document screened in New York City

U.S. Army Lieutenant William Calley convicted of murder for deaths of civilians at My Lai, Vietnam. Verdict later reversed

Concert For Bangla Desh held, New York City

People's Republic of China hosts U.S. table tennis team

Jim Morrison dies

President orders 90-day wage and price freeze and other measures to curb domestic inflation

Bill Graham closes both Fillmore's

People's Republic of China admitted to U.N.

Cyclone and tidal wave kill an estimated ten thousand in Bengal

12.2 million mothers in U.S. labor force

George Jackson dies

Billie Jean King becomes first woman athlete to win $100,000 in one year

Inmate revolt at Attica State Prison

1972

U.S. Senate approved constitutional amendment (E.R.A.) banning sex discrimination; sent to states for ratification

Bangla Desh concert profit of $1,200,000 donated to UNICEF

Governor George C. Wallace, contender for U.S. Democratic presidential nomination, shot while campaigning

Helen Reddy's "I Am Woman" reaches #1

President Nixon visits People's Republic of China and U.S.S.R.

John Lennon's U.S. immigrant visa expires

Washington, D.C. police arrest burglars inside Watergate Democratic National Headquarters

J. Edgar Hoover dies

President Nixon reelected in near record landslide

Michaelangelo's *Pieta* vandalized in St. Peter's Basilica in Rome

U.S. military draft ended; military service becomes voluntary

Arab terrorists responsible for death of eleven Israeli athletes participating in Munich Olympics

U.S. Supreme Court effectively prohibits capital punishment, pending new legislation from states

Joan Baez visits Hanoi during U.S. bombings

Dow Jones Index of stocks closes above 1,000 for first time

Equal Employment Opportunity Act requires equal pay to women for equal work in U.S.

U.S. Environmental Protection Agency announces near-total ban on use of pesticide DDT

Harold S. Geneen, Chairman and President of International Telephone and Telegraph Corporation, receives total annual compensation exceeding 1.6 million dollars

The Tasadays, a stone age tribe, discovered living in caves in Southern Philippines

Nielsen ratings indicate *All in Family,* produced by Norman Lear, most popular U.S. television program

1973

Great Britain, Ireland and Denmark join European Common Market

All state laws limiting a woman's right to an abortion overturned by U.S. Supreme Court

Pablo Picasso dies

American losses in Vietnam War 1965–73: combat deaths 45,948, non-combat deaths 10,298; wounded 303,640

Maximum American troop level during war—1969—543,000; total U.S. expenditures 1965–73: $109.5 billion

U.S. dollar devalued second time in two years

Alan Watts dies

President Nixon ends wage and price controls in all industries except food, health care and construction

U.S.–South Vietnam–North Vietnam–Vietcong cease-fire agreement signed

Marijuana decriminalized in Oregon

Chilean President Salvadore Allende overthrown by military junta

Gram Parsons dies

Energy crisis due to Arab oil embargo and petroleum products shortage

Timothy Leary arrested in Kabul, Afghanistan

Fighting between Arabs and Israelis followed by unstable cease-fire and attempts at peace talks

Clive Davis fired as president of Columbia Records

Terrorism in Northern Ireland; Tower of London and Houses of Parliament bombed by Irish Republican Army

Vice President Agnew resigns, subsequently convicted of income tax evasion. President Nixon names Gerald Ford Vice President

Presidential aides Dean, Haldeman and Erlichman resign under fire

Militant American Indians occupy Wounded Knee, South Dakota

1974

Worldwide inflation heightens

Duke Ellington dies

President Nixon implicated in Watergate break-in cover-up by Administration's tapes of White House conversations. House Judiciary Committee recommends three articles of impeachment for consideration by full House of Representatives. President Nixon resigns. Vice President Gerald Ford becomes 38th President of U.S.

U.S. Secretary of State Henry Kissinger persuades Syria and Israel to agree to cease-fire

Dylan tours U.S.

Floods kill at least 2,500 in Bangla Desh

Picasso's *Guernica* spray-painted at Museum of Modern Art, N.Y.C.

Patti Hearst photographed robbing a bank at age 19

Net profits of 30 of world's largest oil companies increase by an average of 93% during first half of year

President Ford pardons Nixon

President Ford grants limited amnesty to Vietnam War draft evaders and military deserters

U.S. Congress establishes National Institute on Aging

Alexsander Solzhenitsyn, Nobel Prize winning author, expelled by Soviet Union to West Germany

Political kidnappings, bombings and murders become internationally widespread

Record number of natural foods introduced to market

Four Episcopal bishops in U.S. defy church law to ordain eleven women priests

American Telephone and Telegraph Company, largest private U.S. employer, bans discrimination against homosexuals

U.S. Mariner 10 satellite transmits detailed pictures of Venus and Mercury. U.S.S.R. space probe lands on Mars

1975

U.S. military involvement in Vietnam ends. Thousands of South Vietnamese refugees and orphans arrive in U.S.

Violent fighting occurs in Beirut, Lebanon between Palestinian guerrillas and members of Christian right-wing faction

Generalissimo Francisco Franco of Spain dies. Juan Carlos de Borbon y Borbon becomes King Juan Carlos I

Palestinian terrorists disrupt meeting of Organization of Petroleum Exporting Countries (OPEC) in Vienna

N.Y.C. faces financial default; other U.S. cities face similar difficulties

Unemployment rate in U.S. over 9%

Church attendance by all age groups in U.S. reached all-time high of 49% in 1958; reached all time low of 40% during 1971 and 1975

C.I.A. murder plots revealed

Airlift of Vietnamese orphans to U.S. instituted; thousands of Vietnam refugees arrive in U.S.

Provisional Communist government established in South Vietnam

Construction of 789 miles of Alaskan oil pipeline begun

Rolling Thunder Review opens in Plymouth, Mass

President Ford signs tax cut bill. Requests $972 million from Congress for South Vietnam.

Reveals unlawful CIA activities

Kidnap victim and fugitive, Patricia Hearst, captured by F.B.I. agents in San Francisco

U.S. population 213,631,000; per capita income $5,834

Tim Buckley dies

1976

Sal Mineo murdered in Los Angeles

Rubin "Hurricane" Carter released from prison for retrial

Howard Hughes dies

Jimmy Carter elected 39th president

U.S. celebrates bi-centennial

Bob Marley shot in Jamaica

Phil Ochs dies

Gary Gilmore executed, Salt Lake City

Chronologies courtesy of the Whitney Museum of American Art, exhibition materials for *30 Years of American Art: 1945 – 75*, compiled by Barbara Schaefer, Mary Stiles, and Patterson Sims, Curator of exhibition.

Sources

Bob Dylan's career has been well documented, and much of the material on which this book is based comes from the great variety of periodicals, living and dead, that cover the world of rock music. Notable among them are *Rolling Stone, Circus, Crawdaddy, Creem, Cheetah,* and *Fusion. Sing Out! Broadside,* and *Hootenanny* were major sources from the folk period.

Other periodicals consulted included *Life, Look, Time, Newsweek, Playboy, New Musical Express, Los Angeles, KRLA Beat, High Times, Melody Maker, People, Village Voice, East Village Other,* every New York daily paper, *Reader's Digest, Ramparts,* both *Rock* magazines, *Changes, News from Columbia Records, Confidential Flash, Saturday Evening Post, Los Angeles Free Press, Teen Set, National Screw, Teen Screen, Saturday Review,* the only Dylan fanzine—*TBZB/Zimmerman Blues* ($4.00 per year from Zimmerman Blues, c/o Brian Stibal, 4932 Theiss Rd., St. Louis, Missouri 63128), *Radio and Records, Cashbox, Billboard, Record World, Seventeen, Variety, Hi Fi/Stereo Review,* the London *Times,* the *Jerusalem Post, Mademoiselle, Pageant, New York, Cavalier, Vogue, Ingenue, New Yorker, Evergreen, Commentary, Esquire, Commonweal, Eye, American Musical Digest, New Times,* and *TV Guide.*

Books by Bob Dylan complement his prodigious recorded output of twenty legitimate albums, appearances on records by others, and innumerable bootlegs containing enough material to fill twenty-one pages of a computer printout discography prepared by Sandy Gant, the premier Dylan archivist. Dylan also wrote *Tarantula* (Macmillan, New York, 1971), and *Writings and Drawings* (Knopf, New York, 1973), and has released several songbooks including the beautiful *The Songs of Bob Dylan from 1966 through 1975* (Knopf, New York, 1976).

Other books of interest include *Long Time Coming and a Long Time Gone* by Richard Fariña (Random House, New York, 1969); *Song and Dance Man/The Art of Bob Dylan* by Michael Gray (Dutton, New York, 1972); *Bob Dylan* by Daniel Kramer, a photo-study (Castle, New Jersey, 1967); *Bob Dylan, A Retrospective,* a collection of most of the best articles on Dylan in the sixties, edited by Craig McGregor (Morrow, New York, 1972); *Moving Through Here* by Don McNeill (Knopf, New York, 1970); *Bob Dylan Approximately* (McKay, New York, 1975); *Praxis: One* (Book People, Berkeley, 1972), and *Dylan: A Commemoration* (Book People, Berkeley, 1971), a quirky collection of monographs and essays all from Steven Pickering (including much primary source material), concentrating on a mystical Jewish interpretation of *all* Dylan's work, for fanatics only; *Don't Look Back* by D. A. Pennebaker (Ballantine, New York, 1968); *Folk-Rock: The Bob Dylan Story* by Sy and Barbara Ribakove—the earliest Dylan book (Dell, New York, 1966); *Knockin' on Dylan's Door* (Pocket, New York, 1974), a collection of articles on the '74 tour compiled by *Rolling Stone; Bob Dylan* by Anthony Scaduto (Grosset & Dunlap, New York, 1971); *As Time Goes By* by Derek Taylor (Straight Arrow, San Francisco, 1973), a chronicle of the sixties; *Outlaw Blues* by Paul Williams (Dutton, New York, 1969), about the decade's music; and finally, *Positively Main Street* by Toby Thompson, a new-journalism look at Hibbing, personal and fascinating (Coward, McCann & Geoghegan, New York, 1971).

Sam Shepard's *Rolling Thunder Logbook* and journalist Larry Sloman's collection, untitled at this writing, document Dylan's most recent tour. Finally, Robert Shelton, who discovered Bob for the *New York Times* in 1961, has been promising a definitive biography for over a decade.

Overleaf: Photograph by Lynn Goldsmith

several of Neil Young's musicians (along with Young himself), Dylan played guitar, piano, harp, and sang "Are You Ready for the Country," "Ain't That a Lot of Love," several other Young and Band tunes, "Knockin' on Heaven's Door," and "Will the Circle Be Unbroken," the finale, in a performance called reminiscent of the late Sixties. Dylan may have been feeling communal because as soon as he got back to New York, he was again writing songs for a new album, and thinking seriously about another tour.

Jacques Levy, Roger McGuinn's collaborator on "Chestnut Mare" and "Lover of the Bayou," a Ph.D. who'd directed *Oh! Calcutta!,* met Dylan early in 1974 when Bob was writing songs for *Blood on the Tracks.* Levy's relationship with McGuinn had been a complex one, transcending mere friendship or collaboration, and Bob knew of it when they ran into each other on Bleecker Street. He'd just finished his smash tour with The Band and was writing and studying with a New York painter. A year later they met again in approximately the same spot and Levy invited him up to his loft. They began to collaborate together, starting with a song called "Isis," and got so into it they split the city for East Hampton where they holed up for three weeks, writing fourteen songs together. In August Dylan entered the studio in New York with a cast of folk musicians including EmmyLou Harris on backup vocals. It was all live stuff, no overdubs and no second takes. *Desire* was the album's name and it would be released in January '76, just at the end of the Rolling Thunder tour.

Onstage at the Felt Forum, New York, for the Chile benefit concert. *(Waring Abbott/Photo Trends)*

Rolling Thunder was an idea whose time had come. Dylan had thought up the idea in July during a period when he was hanging loose, bopping around the Village wearing the same funky striped shirt, leather jacket, and baggy pants for days on end, seeing shows by Patti Smith, jamming with Jack Elliot at The Other End, with Muddy Waters at The Bottom Line, and with Victoria Spivey at her Brooklyn digs. He played backup on a new David Blue album, shared vocals with Bette Midler on "Buckets of Rain." He also showed up backstage at a Rolling Stones' concert in the Garden. In September he appeared on an educational-TV tribute to John Hammond with Scarlet Rivera, Rob Stoner, and Howie Wyeth. He also recorded another topical song about Rubin "Hurricane" Carter, a heavyweight contender imprisoned in New Jersey after a contradiction-plagued trial for multiple murder.

The single was released when Dylan was three days into his tour, one that had begun with rumors of his playing clubs, and his intentions of playing "to the people."

According to one inside source, Rolling Thunder started out with the image of a club tour for Dylan and Joan Baez, but behind that was an idea for a new Dylan movie, a showbiz extravaganza featuring all of Bob's old friends and new. It would be his production entirely, his money, his friends, his movie. It was a hell of a lot of fun, quite spontaneous. And it began innocently enough that summer when Bobby Neuwirth was playing at The Other End doing his "Budweiser Review" in which anyone in the audience could and did come up and play. Neuwirth was drawing some of the obscure and famous musicians to his act. He was ringleader and Master of Ceremonies to musicians as diverse as Mick Ronson, David Bowie's ex-lead guitarist, to Loudon Wainwright III, an off-the-wall WASP folkie. Ramblin' Jack wandered in and out, sometimes playing, other times yelling comments from the floor.

During the week Neuwirth was working The Other End, Bob and Jacques Levy were sitting in a restaurant next to the club eating a snack. That night Bob played two new songs for the lucky audience, "Joey Gallo" and "Isis," and during the ensuing confusion someone (probably Ramblin' Jack) said to Dylan, "Let's tour." Stranger things can and do happen in the rock and roll world. Elliott went back on tour with his own club dates, only to get a phone call in the middle of his week at Washington's Cellar Door, with the news that the tour was indeed on.

By October, the troops were massing in New York at the Gramercy Park Hotel, with rehearsals for two weeks at Studio Instrument Rentals. It seemed like everyone in the Village scene was around partying and making music, from Ginsberg to J. Paul Getty III. Personalities as diverse as Elliott's Yahoo and Joan Baez's Mannered Mad-Donna were meshing together in a whole that could travel together. Dylan was paying back a lot of debts.

To oversee the tour, Bob brought in his old friend Lou Kemp (described variously as businessman, bodyguard and best buddy). He hired an ex-employee from Bill Graham's organization to plot the logistics, hire a crew and plan the secretive booking of small halls throughout the Northeast. Even as the musicians were playing, getting high, and discussing everything from amplifiers to non-orgasmic housewives, Kemp and his crew were putting things together behind an almost complete wall of secrecy.

Dylan wasn't hiding though; he was on the streets as he had been all summer. These secret new plans almost gave him a cloak of invisibility.

(Lynn Goldsmith)

(Mary Alfieri)

Often he'd walk from the hotel to the rehearsal studio, twenty-five blocks away, guitar in hand, without being noticed. Everyone was impressed by how mellow he'd become. Mellow and still a little weird. One afternoon, for instance, Neuwirth, the ringleader, came running into the studio; he grabbed four or five guys and Dylan to come with him to buy masks at what he called a "goon shop." Dylan asked the proprietor if he had any wigs, describing the kind he wanted, one for a "short guy, thin, long hair." The owner obliged. In a shirt store, Dylan looked at ruffled tux shirts. The storekeeper there asked if he and the boys were from New Jersey or something they looked so strange. No, they were musicians. Name? "Somebody and the Flaming Corks," Dylan replied, deadpan.

Eventually they loaded themselves into a series of buses and campers, blasting off to Plymouth, Massachusetts, for a rehearsal concert in a Cape Cod vacation hotel. The startled middle-agers got the thrill of their children's lives. The opening show was held at the Plymouth Civic Center. Dylan had surrounded himself with some close friends; he was looking to rekindle old creative fires. Among those old firebrands were some of the greatest popular musicians of the Sixties, people who'd given him his start like Baez, Elliott, and Neuwirth, along with other folkie superstars like Eric Andersen, Joni Mitchell, Gordon Lightfoot, and Roger McGuinn. Then there were new musicians, organized by Neuwirth; the band Guam, comprising Mick Ronson, bassist Rob Stoner, T-Bone Burnette, ex-Quacky Duck prodigy David

Bob joined Joan Baez, Phil Ochs, and others at a birthday party for Mike Porco, proprietor of Gerde's Folk City (site of his first professional appearance in 1961), just before the Rolling Thunder tour began. *(Mary Alfieri)*

Mansfield, percussionists, violinists, and even Allen Ginsberg on Harmonium. Ronee Blakley, who'd appeared at one of the Other End jams, impressed Dylan enough to be given a solo spot.

As the tour moved out of Plymouth, into the wilds of New England, playing little burgs like Shelbourne, Vermont, it seemed that the Beatles' dream of a magical mystery tour was coming true. The hotels were in the backwoods, out of the way, and the only visitors were people like Jack Elliott's mother-in-law. Dylan was ensconced in a camper or the Caddy. The troupe was traveling in several buses, sealed off from outsiders, and Ramblin' Jack was thinking about driving either one of the Greyhounds or a semi to all the rest of the dates. Fishing, hanging around, and sitting in the sun making music were the orders of the day.

In Stockbridge, Massachusetts, the troupe checked into the Red Lion Inn and got loose, setting the tone for much of the tour. Neuwirth shouted at two invited guests who entered the bar, "Hey, the hookers are here!" Peculiar white powders were not unknown to the tour group. They were all on a high, self-inflicted or not. While there, they filmed at a club owned by Mama Thorton. "I couldn't believe it," a friend of one of the musicians said, "Dylan was so weird. You could feel his power. If he wanted to, he could stop all the conversation in a room just by moving his head. It was as if everyone was tied to him. Very strange. Very, very, strange. You remember his eyes most of all."

The press were barred from the tour whenever they could be spotted. A reporter from the *Village Voice* was even locked into his hotel room. Neuwirth, the wit, suggested going to a bus station photo booth and taking twenty-five-cent pictures to sell to the photographers who doggedly waited in various hotel lobbies. Security, according to a newspaper in Niagara Falls, was "tight as a drumskin," with cameras and tape recorders being confiscated at the door of each concert by tour personnel. As press paranoia grew, the theory was that Dylan wanted to control the entire output of this tour, allowing only selected journalists access to the performers and only one photographer in the photo pit, along with his own documentary crew. *Rolling Stone* reported that when Dylan was told the meaning of "Rolling Thunder" to Indians ("Speaking Truth"), he replied, "Well, I'm real glad to hear that, man." Most reporters wished he would just speak.

One night Allen Ginsberg shaved his bushy and historical beard for the cameras while McGuinn, a few feet away, danced alone in a rhinestone top hat and black cap, chanting a song. Dylan stood discreetly aside and watched beneath the brim of the cowboy hat he'd worn in the movie *Pat Garrett.* "Artists get temperamental," one of Ramblin' Jack's friends said when a writer was summarily ejected from a hotel party, and it was said as fact, not as apology. The tour was really a private affair and a closed movie set, and people whose jobs entailed the dissemination of information were not invited.

And everything was filmed, whatever went on, whatever they decided to make happen, although when a filmed wrestling match between Dylan and Baez was suggested, Dylan opted out, explaining that a man and woman wrestling just "doesn't look right."

By the time the tour was two weeks old, large halls had become the norm, and complaints about that, and the insular attitude surrounding the production, were bluntly met. Bob told *Rolling Stone* that he never planned to play in people's living rooms. Baez added people could shove it if they didn't like it. Besides it was a hell of an expensive proposition to keep

On an educational TV tribute to John Hammond, Bob performed "Hurricane" with musicians Scarlet Rivera, Rob Stoner, and Howie Wyeth. *(Soundstage/Jon Randolph)*

(Soundstage/Jon Randolph)

The Rolling Thunder Revue (from left): Roger McGuinn, Ramblin' Jack Elliott, Mick Ronson (hidden), Joan Baez, Bob Dylan in whiteface, Bobby Neuwirth in profile and Rob Stoner. *(Paul McAlpine)*

seventy people on the road. Small venues didn't pay that much; business is business.

Audiences didn't care one way or the other. Two shows in Providence, Rhode Island, and two more in New Haven, Connecticut, put seating figures up towards 20,000, and though there were complaints about the rotten sound, they were swamped by the adulation of Dylan's real audience, the kids (some up to forty or fifty years of age) who heard about the tour and moved fast to acquire tickets. Dylan told *People* Magazine he didn't care what people expected of him, but his shows, and the new music presented in them, more than met those expectations.

His shows ran along certain lines, showing that Dylan still knew how to appeal to his audience and their expectations of the unexpected. Like that night in Niagara Falls. After a delay of almost an hour, the Rolling Thunder Review opened with Guam, alternatively known as the Budweiser Review

On December 7 1975, Dylan, Baez, Joni Mitchell, Roberta Flack, and others performed a benefit at New Jersey's Clinton State Prison where Rubin "Hurricane" Carter was serving life sentences for a 1966 multiple murder. Here, Carter greets Dylan, who'd become an advocate for the former middleweight boxer. *(UPI)*

and the Stoner-Neuwirth Band. Flash was apparent as Mick Ronson, the token rocker, immediately commenced using his star guitar moves. It was obvious that his fellow musicians enjoyed it as much as the crowd. Introduced as "a hostage for the revolution," Ronson's playing sparked the hour-long set. Guam was joined at the end by Ronee Blakely for two numbers and then by Joni Mitchell, a surprise guest, for two more. Mitchell, the first star to appear, brought the crowd to its feet, and as she finished, Ramblin' Jack walked on to more delighted screams. Using an electric guitar onstage for the first time in his performing career, the elder statesman of the tour lived up to the almost surprising recognition his name had brought from the audience.

Dylan's appearance, in gray cowboy hat, black vest, a long scarf, eyeliner, and semi-whiteface, turned the arena into a scene of mayhem. As he stormed through "When I Paint My Masterpiece," dedicated to Gertrude Stein and "Mo-Diddly-Anny," the audience settled in for what seemed to be the upcoming loose, fun show.

"It Ain't Me Babe," played as a country shuffle, followed, including Dylan's first harp solo and a fine bit of musicianship from Ronson. An electrified "Hattie Carroll" and "It Takes a Lot to Laugh, It Takes a Train to Cry" confirmed that oldies would not be sacrificed this night. "That was an old song," Bob said to the crowd. "This is a new one," and he blasted into "Durango," from his as-yet unreleased album, *Desire,* an outlaw song filled with studied, introspective arrogance. The crowd roared.

"I hocked my guitar for a few crumbs and a place to hide," Dylan sang, and sure enough, on the next song, "Isis," the guitar was nowhere in evidence as Dylan sang naked in front of the mike, crouched like he was ready to run. The curtain closed and a fifteen-minute intermission saw the remnants of the Sixties' Golden Age mixing with the Seventies' sonic sodbusters as if they'd always been meant for each other. As the curtain rose on Dylan and Baez dueting "Blowin' in the Wind," it was obvious that for these people, the truths of the Sixties had not yet been disproved.

The duets continued with "I Dreamed I Saw St. Augustine," an old Johnny Ace rocker, "Just Let Me Love You Tonight," "Mama You Been on My Mind," and "I Shall Be Released," dedicated to co-writer Richard Manuel of The Band.

Together Dylan and Baez wove a spell that couldn't be broken, and as Baez came to the fore alone for her solo spot, the crystal-voiced spellbinder bound it even tighter. Alternating quasi-standup comedy with songs like "Diamonds and Rust" (about her affair with Dylan) and "Swing Low, Sweet Chariot," she had the hall heated up for Roger McGuinn to sing his single greatest composition from the Late Byrds' years, "Chestnut Mare." Carrying his trademark Rickenbacker guitar and singing in his finest voice in years, McGuinn put into focus the fact that in a way, this tour represented a capsule history of the best years of rock and roll from pre-rockers like Ramblin' Jack to post-rockers like Ronson.

With remarkable perception of the need to pace the show, Dylan returned alone, holding a guitar, harp around his neck, sitting on a stool, for "Love Minus Zero/No Limit," sung in a husky voice that immediately subdued the crowd. When the song was over, though, the crowd began to yell, and as the screams of "DYLAN!" wafted toward the stage, he approached the mike, looked up at the highest balconies, and said, "I think you got me mistaken with someone else." That statement was rendered doubtful as he broke into a reworked version of "Tangled Up in Blue," his blue-gray eyes flashing as brightly as the gold medallion around his neck and the silver watch and ring glinting light from his hand.

With the Band backing him, Dylan soared into another new number, "Oh Sister." Applause met the song in force, causing Dylan to exclaim "My goodness" before breaking into "Hurricane," his just-released single, and "One More Cup of Coffee," a despairing ode of leaving in which Desolation Row is distilled into pure death, inspiring a zealous fan to scream, "Attack the Microphone!" "Sara," a love song to Dylan's wife, who was standing backstage throughout this and many of the shows, came next, followed by "Just Like a Woman" in a kind of reverse story-telling sequence of love and pain. Finally, a majestic "Knocking on Heaven's Door" from the maligned *Pat Garrett* soundtrack and a rousing version of Woody Guthrie's "This Land is Your Land," performed by the entire troup, closed the show. Exhausted and happy after three-and-a-half hours of music, the crowd filtered quietly

(Mary Alfieri)

out of the hall.

"It's a good show, ain't it?" McGuinn asked as he rode up the elevator to the small post-show party. It more than made up for the paranoia that suddenly became the order of business once the troupe had retaken their floor of the Hilton. During the party, some information came out, but mostly it was a gathering of friends, drinking and talking. The next day the film crew and troupe went to an Indian reservation to film a meal featuring dancing, singing, and playing. Then it was back on the road till the final shows a few weeks later, benefits for ex-middleweight contender Carter, jailed, Dylan claimed in song, for a crime he did not commit.

The first "Hurricane" benefit took place December 8, 1976, at Madison Square Garden, with Dylan and Baez finally playing that big hall together. Late in January the troupe, including Kinky Friedman (of the Texas Jewboys) and Ringo Starr, played a second benefit at the Houston Astrodome. The Rolling Thunder Revue remained together on and off through May, when a TV special was taped at the State University of Colorado at Fort Collins, and Dylan's second live album, *Hard Rain,* was taped.

In the year of America's Bicentennial, it seemed as if Bob Dylan and his audience of dreamers, schemers, wise men and fools had finally become an accepted part of the nation's mainstream.

After their Niagara Falls' concerts, Dylan and the Rolling Thunder troupe (including Allen Ginsberg, Ramblin' Jack Elliott and Bobby Neuwirth) spent an afternoon on an Indian reservation in Canada. *(Mary Alfieri)*

Overleaf:
Dylan in Dallas. *(Jesus Carillo)*

Epilogue: On the Road Again

FOR A WHILE it seemed that Dylan's life might be entering a phase of domestic tranquility and artistic explosions. Back with Sara, who'd been on much of the Rolling Thunder Tour, Dylan moved with her and the children into a monstrous house on the beach in Malibu, California, which had been being remodeled for the two years since he had purchased it, to the tune of $2.25 million.

"I had to keep a straight face when Dylan said he wanted a living room he could ride a horse through," architect David Towbin told *Time*. "It would have helped a lot to have been a shrink."

Cashbox reported he'd installed a screening room with the only seating a 1965 Mustang automobile. CBS-TV said the house was sinking into the surf, though Towbin denied it. *Los Angeles* magazine ran a story on it called "Zimmerman's Xanadu."

By September, when *Hard Rain* was aired and the album released, Dylan was at a point of popular success unequaled in his career. He might not have Top 10 singles anymore, but he'd never been on the cover of *TV Guide* before. His interview in that issue was a classic example of media manipulation, Dylan turning the tables on those who'd hurt him, giving 'em what they wanted and getting even more in return. Though his show got lackluster Neilsens, it introduced him to an area of American entertainment previously only touched by such pop acts as Sonny and Cher and John Denver.

The inverview was sly. Dylan chalked it all up to his being a Gemini, which forced him to extreme positions. He still had a lot to do in his life and didn't feel like letting anyone else in on it, even the distinguished correspondent from *TV Guide*. He basically considered himself a musician more than a poet, while his real self was another matter entirely. Above all he hated definitions of any sort; definitions confine actions. Besides there's nothing definite in this world 'cept understanding that if you don't grow you'll die. For himself, he always had to seek new vistas to remain creatively fulfilled.

(Soundstage/Jon Randolph)

On Thanksgiving 1976, Dylan joined The Band at "The Last Waltz," their final concert appearance at San Francisco's Winterland. *(Wide World)*

In January 1977, Jimmy Carter was inaugurated as America's newest president. Through his campaign he'd talked of his friendship with Dylan, whom he'd met briefly while Governor of Georgia. In his inaugural address he said, "We have an America that in Bob Dylan's phrase is busy being born, not busy dying. We will go forward . . . " That same month Dylan was named Songwriter and Composer of 1976 by the readers of *New Musical Express,* Britain's prestigious pop tabloid. Joan Baez released a song directed at Dylan, "O Brother!"

Early in February, Rubin Carter was found guilty of multiple murder for a second time, and sentenced to consecutive life terms. And Dylan, his record company, publisher, and co-author were all reportedly being sued by Penny Valentine, a witness in the case who said she'd been libeled, slandered, and had her privacy invaded by Dylan's use of her name in his song about the boxer. *Rolling Stone* printed a long story by Chet Flippo and Joe Nick Patoski, two Texan journalists, on how the Astrodome Benefit had turned into a giant money-losing shuck. Nothing new came from Dylan, though he'd done a session with, and given a song to, Eric Clapton, and had another session with Leonard Cohen and producer Phil Spector. Plans for the Rolling Thunder movie, a Martin Scorese film of The Band's farewell concert at San Francisco's Winterland the previous Thanksgiving, and a record from that event all remained rumors. At that show, Dylan joined a number of rock luminaries, from Ron Wood to Ronnie Hawkins, playing "Baby Let Me

"Zimmerman's Xanadu." *(Mark Sullivan)*